THE LITERATURE WORKBOOK

THE LITERATURE
WORKBOOK

Clara Calvo
and Jean Jacques Weber

London and New York

First published 1998 by Routledge
11 New Fetter Lane, London EC4P 4EE

Simultaneously published in the USA and Canada
by Routledge
29 West 35th Street, New York, NY 10001

Typeset in Plantin and Gill by Keystroke,
Jacaranda Lodge, Wolverhampton
Printed and bound in Great Britain by
T.J. International Ltd, Padstow, Cornwall

British Library Cataloguing in Publication Data
A catalogue record for this book is available from the British Library

Library of Congress Cataloguing in Publication Data
A catalogue record for this book has been requested

ISBN 0–415–16986–0 (hbk)
ISBN 0–415–16987–9 (pbk)

TO WALTER NASH

CONTENTS

Acknowledgements   xi
Using this book   xiii

1 MINIATURE POEMS
Reading the Elizabethan sonnet as a jewel   1
The age of the sonnet   2
Looking at the miniature case: the Italian and the
English sonnet   6
A poem inside a poem: the final couplet   9
Opening the case: some basic tenets of Petrarchism   11
Convention versus originality   14
Looking into the ornamented case: sonnets and their
subject-matter   19
From the Elizabethan sonnet to the present   23
Re-reading the sonnet   24
Activity and project work   24
References and suggestions for further reading   26

2 WHAT'S SYNTAX GOT TO DO WITH POETRY?
On Puritan mind-style and Romantic world-view   27
Milton's 'When I Consider'   30
Wordsworth's 'The World Is Too Much With Us'   32
Keats' 'To Autumn'   34
Shelley's 'Sonnet to England in 1819'   36
Wordsworth on Milton   37
Activity and project work   38
References and suggestions for further reading   39

3 WOMEN'S POETRY
Same or different?   40
Rewriting mythology: same but different   45
Representing the myth of the Fall: some versions of Eve   47
Activity and project work   51
References and suggestions for further reading   52

4 DEATH ON STAGE

Learning to die in a revenge tragedy 54
Exploiting pathos through language 57
Death and its metaphors 58
Women welcoming death in *The White Devil* 61
The manner of dying in *The Duchess of Malfi* 63
Project work 65
References and suggestions for further reading 66

5 SHERIDAN'S SCHOOL FOR MARRIAGE

The effect of education and the nature of comedy 68
The education of young women 72
Comedy and the confusion of identity 74
Activity and project work 76
References and suggestions for further reading 79

6 DEGENERATE APEMEN OR HEROIC DREAMERS?

On cultural stereotypes and Synge's *The Playboy of the Western World* 80
Colonial stereotypes and the nationalist image 81
How Apeman Paddy was transfigured by the dream, or the new peasant drama 83
Synge's *The Playboy of the Western World* 84
The artist as dreamer 87
Conclusion 87
Activity and project work 88
References and suggestions for further reading 89

7 TALKING ABOUT THE WEATHER

***Emma* and the social web of dialogue** 90
Characterization through dialogue 93
Narrative technique and point of view 98
Dialogue and wit 99
Project work 101
References and suggestions for further reading 103

8 OF ELEPHANTS, SERPENTS AND FAIRY PALACES

Simile and metaphor in Dickens' *Hard Times* 104
Hard Times 105
Gradgrind 107
Metaphors of hair 109
The two meanings of fancy 111
Activity and project work 112
References and suggestions for further reading 115

9 LAUGHTER IN PATRIARCHY AND COLONIALISM
Lexical repetition and Jean Rhys' *Wide Sargasso Sea*   116
Jane Eyre (1847)   117
Of dowries and the right of primogeniture   117
Jean Rhys and *Wide Sargasso Sea* (1966)   118
Colonial and patriarchal implications   122
Conclusion   123
Activity and project work   124
References and suggestions for further reading   125

10 POINT OF VIEW AND ITS EFFECTS
Resisting Brian Moore's *Lies of Silence*   126
Lies of Silence   129
Point of view and characterization   129
Explicit evaluation   130
Implicit evaluation   131
Ideological contradictions in *Lies of Silence*   134
Activity and project work   136
References and suggestions for further reading   137

Glossary   139
Index   145

ACKNOWLEDGEMENTS

The authors would like to thank Talia Rodgers, Sarah Brown, Sophie Powell, Brigid Bell and Jason Arthur for their unfailing support of this project. Acknowledgement is due to the copyright holders of the following material for their kind permission to reprint it here: 'Two Forces': Britannia vs. Anarchy, by Sir John Tenniel, *Punch* 29 October 1881, reproduced with permission of Punch Ltd; an extract from William Faulkner's *The Sound and the Fury*, reproduced with permission of Curtis Brown; 'Leda and the Swan' and an excerpt from 'The Man and the Echo' from *The Collected Works of W. B. Yeats*, Volume I: *The Poems*, revised and edited by Richard J. Finneran, copyright 1928 by Macmillan Publishing Company, copyright renewed (1956 by Georgie Yeats (New York: Scribner, 1997), and an excerpt from *Cathleen ni Hoolihan* from *The Collected Plays of W. B. Yeats*, Revised Edition, copyright 1934, 1952 by Macmillan Publishing Company, copyrights renewed (1962 by Bertha Georgie Yeats and 1980 by Anne Yeats, reprinted with the permission of Scribner, a Division of Simon & Schuster and A. P. Watt Ltd on behalf of Michael Yeats; an extract from 'Tulips' (from 'Ariel' in *Collected Poems*) by Sylvia Plath, reproduced with permission of Faber & Faber and HarperCollins; 'To A Friend Whose Work has Come to Triumph' and an excerpt from 'Old', both from *All My Pretty Ones*, copyright ©1962 by Anne Sexton, renewed 1990 by Linda G. Sexton, reprinted by permission of Sterling Lord Literistic, Inc. and Houghton Mifflin Company, all rights reserved; 'Oh, oh, you will be sorry for that word!' by Edna St Vincent Millay, from *Collected Poems*, HarperCollins, copyright © 1923, 1951 by Edna St Vincent Millay and Norma Millay Ellis, all rights reserved, reprinted by permission of Elizabeth Barnett, literary executor; extracts from *Lies of Silence* by Brian Moore published in 1990 by Bloomsbury Publishing Plc and reprinted with their permission; extracts from *Wide Sargasso Sea* by Jean Rhys, copyright © 1966 by Jean Rhys, reprinted by permission of Penguin Books Ltd and W. W. Norton & Company, Inc.; extract from 'Obeah Night', from *The Letters of Jean Rhys* by Jean Rhys, edited by Francis Wyndham and Diana Melly,

USING THIS BOOK

This book can be used for any introductory course in Literary Studies or Critical Analysis. It can also be used for independent study – though you will find it helpful to discuss the exercises with other people.

The Literature Workbook introduces you to some of the essential analytic and interpretive skills that are needed for literary appreciation and evaluation. It also encourages you to think about historical and cultural issues arising from these concepts and techniques. However, this short textbook cannot hope to introduce you to the huge range of literatures in English. It therefore concentrates mostly on British and Irish literature in English and acquaints you with some of the major practitioners – as well as some less canonical or non-canonical writers. These have been included for the purpose of comparison, and to get you to reflect critically on the concepts of 'literature' and 'the canon'. Last but not least, the book uses a highly practical approach, and each chapter includes a number of activities asking you to apply the new concepts and to develop your understanding of the issues under discussion.

The chapters of the Workbook are arranged according to genre and chronology: the first three chapters deal with poetry, ranging from the Elizabethan sonnet to twentieth-century women's poetry; the three following chapters focus on drama, in particular Jacobean tragedy, eighteenth-century comedy and the drama of the Irish Literary Revival; and the last four chapters look at fiction from Jane Austen and Charles Dickens to Jean Rhys and Brian Moore. Due to restrictions of space, the focus is clearly on the novel, and there is very little on the short story.

The first chapter on the sonnet is considerably longer than the other chapters, because it aims to familiarize you with the remote world of Elizabethan language, literature and culture. Moreover, the poems in this chapter appear in their old-spelling versions, so we have added extensive notes that will help you to work out difficult words and ultimately – we hope – to enjoy reading Elizabethan English.

All the chapters conclude with sections that offer a chance for you to get involved. The exercises in these sections are subdivided into three types:

- Activities, which can be done with the material in the Workbook
- Project Work, which requires you to go beyond the Workbook and to do some extra reading or other research
- For Discussion, which aims to get you to think about some fundamental problems of literary criticism

We do not necessarily expect you to do all these exercises, but we hope that you will choose the ones you are most interested in. A few of them are followed by discussion notes; however, it is important here to remember that we are not dealing with mathematical problems but with fundamentally ambiguous and indeterminate literary texts: our hints and suggestions are really and truly only hints and suggestions intended to make you think about the literary texts, and certainly not the final word on these texts!

A last comment before we embark on our study is that it will be successful only to the extent that it encourages you to read beyond the Workbook itself, to read the whole of the literary texts (novels, plays, poems) discussed in individual chapters. For we must not forget that a very important part in any engagement with literature is our direct, personal response to the primary texts. All *The Literature Workbook* can do is to help you sharpen and articulate this personal response, but it can never be a substitute for it.

I

MINIATURE POEMS
Reading the Elizabethan Sonnet
as a Jewel

In Elizabethan England, miniature portraits were worn as jewels. Miniatures were collected and treasured. They were first hidden in cabinets, in the most private of rooms, the bedroom, and were only shown to intimate friends. When Elizabeth I wanted to single out some foreign ambassador – to indicate, for instance, that his suit would have a chance to progress if he argued it persuasively – she would show him, perhaps to the dismay of competing ambassadors, her collection of miniatures. At first, miniatures were simply kept wrapped in paper. The fondness for display of the Tudor court, however, soon had them taken out of private cabinets. Miniatures, placed inside a very elaborate precious metal case, often adorned with pearls and precious stones, began to be worn as pendants, hanging from chains or ribbons from the neck or the waist. Yet the miniatures themselves, particularly miniatures of one's beloved, remained hidden in their ornamented cases: the Lilliputian portraits were there, within reach, but not to be seen.

The miniature-wearing fashion is parallel in time with the sonnet-writing fashion. In Elizabeth I's court, courtiers wrote sonnets to impress the Queen. The sonnet was, like the miniature, a jewel, an artifice, a display of the poet's ability. Sonnets were not openly displayed, however, since they were not intended for the press and were not published at first. Instead, they circulated in manuscript form for the eyes of a happy few: friends, patrons, lovers. Sonnets, like miniatures, belonged to intimacy. Today, when Elizabethan sonnets can easily be reproduced and obtained, they may still seem to resemble miniatures, as their meaning remains hidden in their beautiful formal cases of quatrains and couplets and complicated rhyme-schemes. Sonnets often express complex thoughts which have been compressed and twisted to fit the well-defined boundaries of fourteen short lines, just as the human portraits in miniatures are artificially confined to a tiny oval shape. This can sometimes prove a very artificial constraint, forcing the poet to make unusual syntactic choices that produce obscure sentences. Sonnets often present difficulty of another sort: just as the white faces of Elizabethan miniatures are usually surrounded by elaborate ruffles, Renaissance sonnets often clothe feelings and ideas in the artifice of Petrarchan love rhetoric. This chapter will aim to show you how to open the richly decorated case, once you have admired it, so that you can see and understand the picture hidden inside.

THE AGE OF THE SONNET

The Renaissance was, in Europe, the Age of the Sonnet. The sonnet appeared first in the Sicilian court of Frederick II, Holy Roman Emperor between 1208 and 1250, and Giacomo da Lentino is the writer who is usually credited with its invention. From Sicily, it went to Italy, and it was the Italian writer Francesco Petrarch who strongly contributed to make it popular. Between 1530 and 1650 there were in Italy, France, Germany and England about 3,000 writers who produced 200,000 sonnets and to this we have to add the Spanish writers and the considerable number of sonnets they wrote until well into the seventeenth century. In England, the sonnet fashion reached its peak between 1580 and 1610. Writers began to produce *sonnet-sequences*, collections of sonnets thoughtfully arranged according to subject-matter, sometimes even spinning a narrative. Sonnet-sequences were sometimes interspersed with other poems or 'songs', as in Sir Philip Sidney's *Astrophil and Stella*, or they could be followed by a long poem placed at the end of the sequence, as in Samuel Daniel's *Delia*, Spenser's *Amoretti* and, possibly, Shakespeare's *Sonnets*. A curious version of the sonnet-sequence is the *crown sequence*, as in Lady Mary Wroth's *Pamphilia to Amphilanthus*, which includes a sonnet-sequence in which each new sonnet begins by repeating the last line of the previous sonnet and the last sonnet ends with the first sonnet's first line.

sonnet-sequence

crown sequence

In Tudor England, the sonnet soon became a useful tool to move within the system of patronage – and this can partly explain its success amongst those close to the crown or willing to please noble patrons. The sixteenth-century courtier does not need to give counsel or advice to the monarch. He needs instead to please, to make himself agreeable in order to be first on the monarch's list for a post or a privilege. One way of achieving this is to display one's artistic abilities. It is hardly surprising therefore that the first sonnets in England are the work of two courtiers and aristocrats: Sir Thomas Wyatt (1503?–42) and Henry Howard, Earl of Surrey (1517?–47), both of whom lived and wrote in the reign of Henry VIII. Neither Wyatt nor Surrey published their poems, but they appeared in a collection of 'songes and sonettes' by several authors which is known today by the name of *Tottle's Miscellany* (1557). *Tottle's Miscellany* contains fifteen sonnets by Surrey and twenty-seven by Wyatt.

a) **Compare the following two sonnets by Wyatt and Surrey and jot down some notes about their differences regarding their subject-matter and their rhyme patterns.**

b) Renaissance sonnets are often accused of being artificial, static, hieratic (like the faces in the miniatures which have no wrinkles or lines). They are seen as expressing not real feeling but idealized emotions. To what extent does this apply to the following two poems?

Sir Thomas Wyatt

Who so list to hount I knowe where is an hynde
but as for me helas I may no more
the vayne travaill hath weried me so sore
I ame of theim that farthest cometh behinde
yet may I by no meanes my weried mynde
drawe from the Deere but as she fleeth afore
faynting I folowe I leve of therefor
sethens in a nett I seke to hold the wynde
Who list her hount I put him owte of dowbte
as well as I may spend his tyme in vain
and graven with Diamondes in letters plain
There is written her faier neck rounde abowte
noli me tangere for Cesars I ame
and wylde for to hold though I seme tame

GLOSSARY

line 1   *Who so* Whoever; *list* likes, wishes; *hount* hunt; *hynde* hind
line 2   *helas* alas; *may* can
line 3   *vayne travaill* vain effort; *weried* wearied; *so sore* so much
line 4   *theim* them; *cometh* comes
line 5   *meanes* means; *mynde* mind
line 6   *drawe* withdraw; *Deere* deer (and dear); *fleeth* flees; *afore* in front
line 7   *faynting* fainting; *folowe* follow; *leve of* leave, stop
line 8   *sethens* since; *nett* net; *seke* seek, try; *wynde* wind
line 9   *owte of dowbte* out of doubt
line 11 *graven* engraven
line 12 *faier* fair; *abowte* about
line 13 *noli me tangere for Cesars I ame* do not touch me because I belong to the King; *noli me tangere* were the words Christ addressed to Mary Magdalene after the Resurrection (see John 20:17) but they are also said to have been the motto which Caesar's deer wore in their collars to keep hunters away; *Cesars I ame* echoes the gospel 'Render therefore unto Caesar the things which are Caesar's' (Matthew 22:21).
line 14 *wylde* wild; *seme* seem

Henry Howard, Earl of Surrey

Norfolk sprang thee, Lambeth holds thee dead,
Clere of the County of Cleremont though hight.
Within the wombe of Ormondes race thou bread
And sawest thy cosin crowned in thy sight;
Shelton for love, Surrey for Lord thou chase,
Ay me, while life did last, that league was tender:
Tracing whose steps thou sawst Kelsall blaze,
Laundersey burnt, and battered Bullen render,
At Muttrell gates hopeles of all recure,
Thine Earle halfe dead gave in thy hand his will:
Which cause did thee this pining death procure,
Ere summers four times seaven, thou couldest fulfill.
Ah, Clere, if love had booted, care, or cost;
Heaven had not wonn, nor earth so timely lost.

GLOSSARY

line 1	*sprang* gave birth to; *thee* you; *holds thee dead* Clere was buried in Lambeth
line 2	*though hight* though called (your name is Cleremont although you are called Clere)
line 3	*within the wombe of Ormondes race thou bread* Clere was born ('bread' i.e. bred) in the Ormond family
line 4	*sawest* saw; *thy cosin* your cousin; Anne Boleyn, who married Henry VIII and was crowned in 1533, was Clere's relative.
line 5	*Shelton* Clere's wife was Mary Shelton; *thou* you; *chase* chose
line 6	*league* bond, relationship (between Surrey and Clere)
line 7	*Tracing whose steps* Clere followed Surrey's steps by going to war in his military retinue; Kelsall (Scotland) was burnt by the English in 1542
line 8	*Laundersey* Landrecy (France) underwent siege in 1543; *render* surrender
lines 8–9	*Bullen . . . Muttrell* Boulogne . . . Montreuil
line 9	*hopeles* hopeless; *recure* recovery
line 12	*ere* before; *summers four times seaven, thou couldest fulfill* you could be twenty-eight years old
line 13	*booted* been of help, availed, provided help
line 14	*wonn* won

DISCUSSION   a) With regard to subject-matter, the only similarity between these two sonnets is that they both regret the 'absence' of a person, the impossibility of enjoying the company of someone the poet loves: Wyatt laments that Anne Boleyn is beyond his reach since the King takes an interest in her; Surrey mourns the death of his friend Clere. There are several differences: Wyatt's is a love poem; Surrey's is an elegy, a lament for someone's death. Wyatt uses an extended metaphor: deer – beloved – Anne Boleyn; hunter – lover – Wyatt himself; hunting – courting. Surrey is very sparse with metaphor, though he does use *personification* (a figure of speech in which inanimate objects or abstract entities are given human attributes): 'Norfolk sprang thee, Lambeth holds thee dead'; 'Heaven had not wonn, nor earth so timely lost'. With regard to rhyme-schemes, these sonnets have one thing in common: they both end with a couplet, a pair of lines which share the same rhyme. In a sonnet, this pair of rhyming lines is called the *final couplet*. However, these sonnets are different with regard to the remaining twelve lines: Wyatt's sonnet rhymes **abba abba cddc ee** whereas Surrey's rhymes **abab cdcd efef gg**.

personification

final couplet

b) Artificiality in shape through rhetorical means should not be confused with artificiality in content, in the emotions expressed. Both of these sonnets are highly rhetorical and in that sense 'artificial' but the emotions are described in such a way that it is not difficult to believe that they have been sincerely felt. Wyatt's feeling of exhaustion, of being tired out by his 'chase' after Anne Boleyn is cleverly conveyed through the insistent presence of expressions reminding us of his state: 'helas I may no more' (l. 2), 'the vayne travaill hath weried me' (l. 3), 'I ame of theim that farthest cometh behinde' (l. 4), 'my weried mynde' (l. 5), 'faynting I folowe' (l. 7), 'as well as I may spend his tyme in vain' (l. 10). All these expressions of tiredness which are scattered throughout the sonnet help to build an image of Wyatt as a lover who is so tired (physically and emotionally) of not getting very far that he has decided to give up. Just when we believe it is Anne Boleyn, cast in the role of disdainful lady, whom Wyatt blames for his exhaustion, then comes the surprise: it is not Anne but Henry VIII who is responsible for Wyatt's present state. Wyatt might well be tired of pursuing somebody who belongs to the English monarch. By giving a powerful reason for the unattainability of the loved one, Wyatt manages to sound more sincere than other Renaissance sonneteers. In Surrey's sonnet, emotions sound just as sincere if not more. Surrey's exclamation in line 6 ('Ay me, while life did last, that league was tender') is wedged into the natural syntactic structure of the sentence ('Shelton for love, Surrey for Lord thou chase,/ . . . Tracing whose steps thou sawst Kelsall blaze') as if the poet had not been able to restrain a sigh of sorrow. Surrey's sonnet also conveys clearly felt admiration for Clere's valour in running to succour the dying earl (ll. 10–11) and the final couplet, serving almost as an epitaph, again expresses deep-felt emotion: Surrey, addressing his dead friend, tells him that if he could have done anything to prevent it, Clere would not now be in heaven, he would still be among the living.

LOOKING
AT THE
MINIATURE
CASE: THE
ITALIAN AND
THE ENGLISH
SONNET

**Petrarchan
sonnet**

Wyatt was the first to translate and write sonnets in English. At first his sonnets were translations of Petrarch's sonnets, but he was soon writing sonnets of his own, in imitation of those he had translated. When Wyatt introduces the sonnet in England, the sonnet has already been completely accepted in Italy as the ideal form for a love poem. Petrarch has already produced his sonnets to Laura in his *Rime sparse* or *Canzoniere* (1470), a sequence of short poems in which the poet describes his ideal love for an unattainable lady. Each sonnet has fourteen lines and is divided into two stanzas: an octave (consisting of eight lines) and a sestet (consisting of six lines). The octave is further subdivided into two four-line quatrains and the sestet into two three-line tercets. The rhyme-scheme of the poems is usually **abba abba cde cde** or **abba abba cdc dcd**.

In the Petrarchan sonnet, the main break or division of the poem occurs between the octave and the sestet and there are two common ways of blending this fixed form with its content:

♦ The octave can express the first part or the first half of an idea and the sestet can provide the second part or second half of the same idea; the sestet can thus be used to expand on an idea, often by means of a copulative conjunction such as *and* or a consecutive conjunction such as *then*. (Shakespeare's sonnet 144 is an example of the first way of linking the first two quatrains with the remainder of the sonnet and Sidney's sonnet 31 in *Astrophil and Stella* is an example of the second.)

♦ Alternatively, the octave can propound an argument and the sestet can proceed to attack or criticise it: as in certain kinds of syllogisms, the octave is reserved for the thesis and the sestet for the antithesis. The sestet's function is then to introduce a new thought or a new development of the thought, often by means of an adversative conjunction such as *but*. (There is an example of this other way of linking octave and sestet in the opening sonnet of Sidney's *Astrophil and Stella*, where line 9 reads: 'But wordes came halting forth, wanting Inventions stay'.)

In some of his sonnets, Wyatt altered the form and the structure of the Petrarchan sonnet: he changed the sestet into one quatrain and one couplet (4+2=6) and the final couplet (the last two lines sharing the same rhyme) became one of the most distinctive features of what has since been referred to as the 'English Sonnet', to distinguish it from the Petrarchan or 'Italian Sonnet'. The change in the stanzaic structure of the sonnet brought along a change in rhyme structure. In the Italian sonnet, the rhyme scheme was quite strict:

♦ the octave always rhymes **abba abba** (*rima chiusa*)
♦ the sestet rhymes **cde cde** or **cdc cdc** (*rima incatenata*).

Sometimes other rhyme-schemes can be found for the sestet but these are the most frequent. The presence of the final couplet altered the rhyme pattern, so the sonnet-form used by Wyatt often rhymed like this: **abba abba cddc ee** or **abba abba cdcd ee**. Wyatt's sonnet form, however, still retains an important characteristic of the Italian sonnet: the repetition of the same rhyme pattern in the first and second quatrains, which created unity for the octave.

The Earl of Surrey is often thought of as one of the first poets to use the type of metre that would become most successful in English poetry, the *iambic pentameter*. A metre is a fixed arrangement of stressed and unstressed syllables into units called feet. Surrey used strings of iambic pentameters with no rhyme (blank verse) in his translation of Virgil's *Aeneid* and he also used this metre in some of his sonnets, as in the one quoted below; but its success in English poetry is probably due to the work of Sidney, Spenser and Shakespeare. The iambic pentameter provides the Elizabethan sonnet with its particular 'pace', its familiar discursive rhythm:

iambic pentameter

And thus I see among these pleasant thinges
Eche care decayes, and yet my sorow springes.

If one tries to count how many stressed and unstressed syllables there are in each line of this couplet, which belongs to a sonnet written by Surrey, one can see that he uses the iambic pentameter here. This metre is composed of five iambic feet, each foot consisting of one unstressed syllable (⌣) followed by a stressed one (-):

/ And thus / I see / a - mong / these plea - / sant things /
/ ⌣ - / ⌣ - / ⌣ - / ⌣ - / ⌣ - /

/ Eche care / de - cayes, / and yet / my sor - / ow springes /
/ ⌣ - / ⌣ - / ⌣ - / ⌣ - / ⌣ - /

Surrey also contributed to the alteration of the shape of the sonnet: he is often credited with having established the basic form of the most successful rhyme pattern used in the sonnets written in England – the rhyme-scheme which Shakespeare used in his own sonnet-sequence, **abab cdcd efef gg**. Surrey gave new rhymes to the second quatrain, and he also changed the rhyming pattern from **abba** to **abab** (alternating rhymes). This English or, as it is also called, *Shakespearean sonnet* has then seven different rhymes, instead of just four or five, as in the Italian, the French and the Spanish sonnet. Reasons have been sought for Surrey's alteration of the rhyming scheme used by the Italian sonnet. One reason could be that Italian offers many words which rhyme and the rhyming scheme was relatively easy to achieve, whereas English, instead, is a language which poses great difficulties to a poet looking for words which rhyme with each other, particularly for 'full' rhyme, and this probably led Surrey to alter the sonnet's rhyming scheme.

Shakespearean sonnet

However, with regard to rhyme and rhyme patterns, it is best to regard the Renaissance sonnet as a site of experimentation: many different rhyme-schemes seem to have been used by different writers (the sonnets reproduced in this chapter make a varied sampler) and some writers seem to have considered it important to vary the rhyme pattern from one sonnet to the next in a sonnet-sequence. Surrey himself did a great deal of experimenting with rhyme patterns, as the following sonnet shows:

Henry Howard, Earl of Surrey

The soote season, that bud and blome furth bringes,
With grene hath clad the hill and eke the vale:
The nightingale with fethers new she singes:
The turtle to her make hath tolde her tale:
Somer is come, for every spray nowe springes,
The hart hath hong his olde hed on the pale:
The buck in brake his winter cote he flinges:
The fishes flote with newe repaired scale:
The adder all her sloughe awaye she slinges:
The swift swalow pursueth the flyes smale:
The busy bee her honye now she minges:
Winter is worne that was the flowers bale:
And thus I see among these pleasant thinges
Eche care decayes, and yet my sorow springes

GLOSSARY

line 1 *soote* sweet; *furth* forth; *bringes* brings
line 2 *grene* green; *hath* has; *eke* also; *vale* valley
line 3 *fethers* feathers; *singes* sings
line 4 *turtle* turtle dove; *make* mate, breeding-partner; *tolde* told
line 5 *somer* summer; *spray* sprig; *nowe* now; *springes* springs, comes out
line 6 *hart* male deer; *hong* hung; *hed* head (i.e. the hart's antlers, which are shed annually); *pale* stake, a pointed piece of wood used to build a fence
line 7 *buck* male deer or rabbit; *brake* thicket, brushwood; *cote* coat; *flinges* throws away
line 8 *The fishes flote* the fish float (i.e. swim); *newe* new
line 9 *slough* skin; *awaye* away; *slinges* slings, discards
line 10 *swalow* swallow; *pursueth* pursues; *flyes* flies; *smale* small
line 11 *honye* honey; *minges* mixes, remembers
line 12 *worne* worn, gone; *bale* harm, evil
line 13 *thinges* things
line 14 *Eche* each; *decayes* decays; *sorow* sorrow

With the new alternating rhymes, the poet also has a choice to place the turn after the second quatrain (after the 'octave') or after the third quatrain, as Surrey did in the sonnet just quoted. If the poet chooses this second option, the former unity of the octave, which in Wyatt's sonnets still remains in the cohesion of the **abba abba** rhyme scheme, now tends to disappear: the octave and sestet have totally metamorphosed into three quatrains and a couplet. The new structure has, however, its own advantages: the poet can place the turning point in the sonnet's subject-matter just before the final couplet and this enhances the epigrammatic quality of the couplet. The couplet of the English sonnet is a miniature inside another miniature: a poem inside another poem.

The final couplet turned out to be very successful and has become one of the distinguishing features of the English sonnet. This final couplet often has the quality of an epigram, slightly independent from the rest of the poem. It tends to encapsulate a thought, a conclusion reached after a good deal of thinking, a resolution. The final couplet functions then as a sort of summary of the entire poem; it is a conclusion, a *dénouement*, but it also frequently expresses a moral, a piece of advice, a maxim of conduct which is easily extracted from the poem and applicable to other situations or human beings. In this, the final couplet is related to a favourite genre in Renaissance literature: the proverb, the maxim, the sententia, the apothegm. The sonnet can also be related to two other Renaissance literary genres: the essay, as cultivated by Montaigne and Bacon, and the emblem. Emblems were composed of three parts: a phrase or motto (often in Latin and of a cryptic nature), a picture, and a poem explaining the relation between the phrase and the picture. The final couplet of the sonnet, like the motto in an emblem, offers the quintessence of a thought.

A POEM INSIDE A POEM: THE FINAL COUPLET

Finally, the advantage of the final couplet is that the poet can give the poem a humorous or ingenious ending. Wyatt's successors exploited this possibility and by doing so they could mix the gravity or seriousness of a topic with touches of wit and humour. This was part of the spirit of the Italian sonnet: the sonnet had to blend *gravità* (seriousness, earnestness) with *dolcezza* (sweetness, gentleness, mildness). Michael Drayton (1563–1631), in a sonnet from his sonnet sequence *Idea* (1594), mixes these two qualities in the three quatrains and produces a witty couplet to round it off.

gravità dolcezza

Michael Drayton, *Idea*, Sonnet 61

Since ther's no helpe, Come let us kisse and part,
Nay, I have done: you get no more of Me,
And I am glad, yea glad with all my heart,
That thus so cleanly, I my Selfe can free,
Shake hands for ever, Cancell all our Vowes,
And when We meet at any time againe,
Be it not seene in either of our Browes,
That We one jot of former Love reteyne;

Now at the last gaspe, of Loves latest Breath,
When his Pulse fayling, Passion speechlesse lies
When Faith is kneeling by his bed of Death,
And Innocence is closing up his Eyes,
  Now if thou would'st, when all have given him over,
  From Death to Life, thou might'st him yet recover.

GLOSSARY

line 1   *ther's* there is
line 2   *Nay* no
line 3   *yea* yes
line 5   *Vowes* vows, promises
line 7   *seene* seen; *Browes* brows, foreheads
line 8   *reteyne* retain
line 9   *gaspe* gasp; *of Loves* of Love's
line 10   *fayling* failing; *speechlesse* speechless
line 13   *would'st* (wouldest) would, wished to
line 14   *might'st* (mightest) might

This sonnet is rather unusual because it contains two structural turns, the first at the beginning of line 9 ('Now at the last gaspe') and the second at the beginning of the final couplet in line 13 ('Now if thou would'st'). The first two quatrains form a sort of 'octave' in which the poets speaks in a light-hearted, gentle tone (*dolcezza*) whereas the third quatrain offers a change in the direction of serious thoughts (*gravità*). However, even in this sonnet with two turns, the definitive turning is reserved for the final couplet which aims, above all, to take you by surprise. The idea expressed in the couplet contradicts everything else previously said in the sonnet: we thought the poet was aiming to put an end to his love relationship with as little emotional cost as possible and in the last line, when the sonnet is about to end – and therefore to 'die' – we find out that he is telling his lover, 'let's try again'.

John Donne (1572–1631) has also mixed seriousness and wit in a well-known sonnet on death whose first two lines read: 'Death, be not proud, though some have called thee/ Mighty and dreadfull, for, thou art not soe'. The final couplet in this sonnet is amongst the most astonishing in English literature. The couplet is remarkable because it postpones the turn of the sonnet until *just* four words before the end:

One short sleepe past, wee wake eternally,
And death shall be no more; death, thou shalt die.

In this final couplet addressed to death itself, Donne has clearly shown the possibilities for compactness, for the tight packaging of ideas, which the final couplet offers.

The English Renaissance sonnet often took the shape of a little love poem; following the trend popularised by Petrarch, many sonnets were written according to the artificial code of Renaissance love rhetoric. Just as the miniatures presented a picture in its case, sonnets written in the Petrarchan fashion often offered feelings framed in the artifice of a number of shared poetic conventions. Some of these conventions are exploited in a well-known miniature by the English painter Nicholas Hilliard, *Man Against a Background of Flames*, painted *c*.1595. This miniature shows the portrait of a lover and the background to the picture is entirely covered with flames. This suggests that the man is being portrayed as a lover: a lover who is burning because, as Petrarchan rhetoric dictates, love is fire and passion burns. In Petrarchan sonnets, lovers usually lament their sad fate, which is to love without being loved in return. The Petrarchan lover, both in the miniature and in Renaissance sonnets, is represented as someone who burns in his own unrequited passion.

OPENING THE CASE: SOME BASIC TENETS OF PETRARCHISM

Miniatures and sonnets were often exchanged between lovers as love tokens: we can assume that this miniature was painted with the intention of giving it to the man's beloved. In Hilliard's portrait, in fact, the man is also depicted as wearing a miniature, which is hanging from a chain around his neck (his hand is holding it so that we do not fail to notice it). This miniature he is wearing is possibly his mistress's portrait, so he is giving her a miniature which contains his portrait wearing a portrait of herself. More importantly, her portrait, hanging from a chain, symbolizes that he is chained to his lady, he cannot get away from her because his love has made him a prisoner, which is another fundamental ingredient of Petrarchism. The chain also symbolizes fidelity: the lover depicted here is claiming that he is faithful to his lady. The portrait thus makes use of several of the *topoi*, the commonplaces of Petrarchism: unrequited love, the lover who cannot stop loving even though he is burning in his own passion, love as pain, love as passion stronger than will, the lover who is chained to his love, the lover's fidelity to his lady. Other commonplaces of Petrarchism are the use of *oxymoron* (love is a 'freezing' fire), love as a labyrinth and the power of love to transcend death: love is stronger than death, love is immortal. These are topics which became part of a shared European culture, the highly rhetorical language of Renaissance love poems, and will appear again and again, with greater or lesser success, in English sonnets throughout the Renaissance. Lady Mary Wroth (1586?–1653?), writing at the end of the period, still makes use of Petrarchan conventions and ends her crown sequence with a couplet which echoes the condition of the Petrarchan lover, a prisoner burning in fire:

topoi ⟵

oxymoron ⟵

Soe though in Love I fervently doe burne,
In this strange labourinth how shall I turne?

The representation of the lover as burning in the passion of love logically leads to an image of love as a painful experience. The idea of love as endless pain and misery is common to sonnets and other Renaissance love poems, including the lyrics of many lute songs. Much of the following sonnet, which Richard Barnfield (1574–1627) wrote for his sonnet-sequence *Cynthia* (1595), is dedicated to depicting love as suffering, as a painful emotion or, to use an Elizabethan expression, as a 'dolefull state':

Richard Barnfield, *Cynthia*, Sonnet 11

Sighing, and sadly sitting by my Love,
　　He ask't the cause of my hearts sorrowing,
　　Conjuring me by heavens eternall King
To tell the cause which me so much did move.
Compell'd: (quoth I) to thee I will confesse,
　　Love is the cause; and onely love it is
　　That doth deprive me of my heavenly blisse.
Love is the paine that doth my heart oppresse.
And what is she (quoth he) whom thou do'st love?
　　Looke in this glasse (quoth I) there shalt thou see
　　The perfect forme of my faelicitie.
When, thinking that it would strange Magique prove,
　　He open'd it: and taking off the cover,
　　He straight perceav'd himselfe to be my Lover.

GLOSSARY

line 2　*ask't* asked; *my hearts* my heart's
line 3　*eternall* eternal
line 5　*Compell'd* compelled; *quoth* said; *confesse* confess
line 6　*onely* only
line 7　*doth* does; *blisse* bliss, happiness
line 8　*oppresse* oppress
line 9　*do'st* (doest) do
line 10　*Looke* look; *glasse* glass, mirror; *shalt* shall
line 11　*forme* form; *faelicitie* felicity
line 12　*Magique* magic, witchcraft
line 14　*straight* straight away; *perceav'd* perceived, realised; *himselfe* himself

a) **Single out all the expressions in the sonnet which have to do with pain or misery and begin to build up your own personal lexicon of Petrarchan images of love.**
b) **Being a Renaissance text, this sonnet is unusual because it gives a voice to same-sex desire. How do we know this? How is gender encoded in the text of this sonnet?**

DISCUSSION

a) Expressions dealing with pain and suffering are numerous in the first two quatrains or octave, but they are absent from the third quatrain and the final couplet. The experience of painful emotions is conveyed through the following lexical choices: 'Sighing, and sadly sitting' (l. 1), 'my hearts sorrowing' (l. 2), 'the cause which me so much did move' (l. 4), 'deprive me of my heavenly blisse' (l. 7) and 'the paine that doth my heart oppresse' (l. 8). The last line in the octave neatly condenses the central idea of the first half of the sonnet: love means pain, to love is to suffer.

b) *Gender* is here encoded through the third-person pronouns 'she' and 'he', particularly in lines 2, 9, 13 and 14. The person addressed in the sonnet is male ('He ask't', l. 2) and he assumes the poet's persona (the 'I' in the poem) will have a female lover ('she . . . whom thou do'st love', l. 9). Whether this 'I' is assumed to be male or female, the sonnet contemplates the existence of same-sex love. Since other sonnets in the sequence enable us to read the 'I' in the poem as male, the poem thus presents a scene of male homo-erotic desire.

gender

Petrarchan rhetoric is very fond of bringing contraries together, so Petrarchan love also had to have its pleasant sides. Sonnets do sometimes portray the condition of being in love as a pleasant, enjoyable pursuit. The following sonnet depicts love as contemplation: the lover takes delight in thinking about love. This convention of presenting the lover as taking delight in a contemplative life, mostly occupied with thinking about the loved one, has led to the image of the Petrarchan lover as a solitary individual who loathes the company of other human beings, a stereotype which has been parodied both by Shakespeare in *Romeo and Juliet* and by Cervantes in *Don Quixote*. When it fell into good hands, such as those of Lady Mary Wroth who wrote the sonnet-sequence *Pamphilia to Amphilanthus* (1621), the topic could be turned into a reminder of the pleasure to be had in intellectual occupation and a beautiful eulogy of the life of the mind.

Lady Mary Wroth, *Pamphilia to Amphilanthus*, Sonnet 23

When every one to pleasing pastimes hies
some hunt, some hauke, some play, while some delight
in sweet discourse, and musique showes joys might
yett I my thoughts doe farr above thes prise.
The joy which I take, is that free from eyes
I sitt, and wunder att this daylike night
soe to dispose them-selves, as voyd of right;
and leave true pleasure for poore vanities;
When others hunt, my thoughts I have in chase;

if hauke, my minde att wished end doth fly,
discourse, I with my spiritt tauke, and cry
while others, musique is theyr greatest grace.
O God, say I, can thes fond pleasures move?
Or musique bee butt in deere thoughts of love?

GLOSSARY

line 1   *hies* goes, hurries
line 2   *hauke* hawk, hunt with a hawk
line 3   *showes* shows; *joys might* the might (power) of joy
line 4   *yett* yet; *doe* do; *farr* far; *thes* these (the 'pleasing pastimes'); *prise* prize
line 6   *sitt* sit; *wunder* wonder; *att* at
line 7   *voyd* empty, devoid
line 11   *spiritt* spirit; *tauke* take
line 12   *theyr* their
line 14   *bee* be; *butt* but, except; *deere* dear

CONVENTION VERSUS ORIGINALITY

Perhaps, the better known Petrarchan commonplace is the praise of the lover's lady: a Petrarchan lady has to have a fair skin, rosy cheeks, ruby-red lips, super-blond hair, a long white neck, sweet breath and a delicious smell. The following sonnet by Edmund Spenser (1552?–99), included in his sonnet sequence *Amoretti* (1595), is a variation on this theme:

Edmund Spenser, *Amoretti*, Sonnet 64

Comming to kisse her lyps, (such grace I found)
Me seemd I smelt a gardin of sweet flowres:
that dainty odours from them threw around
for damzels fit to decke their lovers bowres.
Her lips did smell lyke unto Gillyflowers,
her ruddy cheekes lyke unto Roses red:
her snowy brows lyke budded Bellamoures,
her lovely eyes like Pincks but newly spred,
Her goodly bosome lyke a Strawberry bed,
her neck lyke to a bounch of Cullambynes:
Her brest lyke lillyes, ere theyr leaves be shed,
her nipples lyke yong blossomd Jessemynes.
Such fragrant flowres doe give most odorous smell,
but her sweet odour did them all excell.

GLOSSARY

line 1   *lyps* lips
line 2   *Me seemd* it seemed to me; *gardin* garden; *flowres* flowers
line 4   *damzels* damsels, young single women; *their lovers bowres* their lover's bowers

line 5   *lyke* like; *Gillyflowers*, sweet-scented flowers, similar to pinks
line 7   *Bellamoures* a type of white flower
line 8   *Pincks* pinks; *spred* spread, opened out
line 9   *bosome* bosom
line 10   *bounch* bunch; *Cullambynes* columbines, a plant with pink
          flowers
line 11   *brest* breast; *ere* before; *lillyes*, lilies
line 12   *yong* young; *blossomd* blossomed; *Jessemynes* jasmins

a) **There is something rather artificial about the form, the 'outward case' of this
   sonnet: can you spot it? To what extent is Spenser's technique of fragmenting
   the female body into separate body parts reminiscent of pornographic
   literature?**

Despite the idealized image of the loved one which Spenser's sonnet
presents, by comparing each part of the lady's body to a different type
of flower, it makes at least an effort to improve on the stereotypical
Petrarchan female portrait which was often mechanically reproduced
in many Renaissance poems, such as the following one, written by
Thomas Watson (1557?–92) and included in his *Hecatompathia, or the
Passionate Century of Love* (1582).

Thomas Watson, *Hecatompathia* 7

Harke you that list to heare what sainte I serve:
Her yellow lockes exceede the beaten goulde;
Her sparkeling eies in heav'n a place deserve;
Her forehead high and faire of comely moulde;
Her wordes are musicke all of silver sounde;
Her wit so sharpe as like as can scarce be found;
Each eyebrowe hanges like Iris in the skies;
Her Eagles nose is straight of stately frame;
On either cheeke a Rose and Lillie lies;
Her breath is sweete perfume, or hollie flame;
Her lips more red than any Corall stone;
Her necke more white, than aged Swans that mone;
Her brest transparent is, like Christall rocke;
Her fingers long, fit for Apolloes Lute;
Her slipper such as Momus dare not mocke;
Her vertues all so great as make me mute:
What other partes she hath I neede not say,
Whose face alone is cause of my decaye.

GLOSSARY

line 1   *Harke you that list to heare* listen you who desire or wish to
          hear
line 2   *goulde* gold

line 3   *sparkeling eies* sparkling eyes
line 6   *scarce* scarcely, hardly
line 7   *hanges like Iris in the skies* Iris, a messenger of the Gods, personified the rainbow in Greek mythology and is usually portrayed with wings. 'Iris' is used here as a poetic name for 'rainbow', so each eyebrow of the poet's lady is a perfect semicircular arch, like a rainbow
line 8   *Eagles* eagle's
line 10   *hollie* holy
line 11   *Corall* coral
line 12   *mone* moan
line 13   *Christall* crystal
line 14   *Apolloes* Apollo's
line 15   *Momus* Greek god of ridicule
line 16   *vertues* virtues

b) Is this a sonnet? Do you find that the praise of the beloved is overdone in Watson's poem? Why or why not? How serious or witty is the praise intended to be? (Read the final couplet again.)

William Shakespeare (1564–1616) also included a description of his lady in his sonnet sequence (written 1593–6; published 1609), but it is somehow very different from either Spenser's or Watson's orthodox Petrarchan female portraits.

William Shakespeare, *Sonnet* 130

My Mistres eyes are nothing like the Sunne;
Currall is farre more red than her lips red;
If snow be white, why then her brests are dun;
If haires be wiers, black wiers grow on her head.
I have seene Roses damaskt, red and white,
But no such Roses see I in her cheekes,
And in some perfumes is there more delight
Than in the breath that from my Mistres reekes.
I love to heare her speake, yet well I know
That Musicke hath a farre more pleasing sound.
I graunt I never saw a goddesse goe,
My Mistres when shee walkes treads on the ground.
And yet, by heaven, I thinke my love as rare,
As any she beli'd with false compare.

GLOSSARY

line 1   *Mistres eyes* mistress's eyes
line 2   *Currall* coral; *farre* far
line 3   *dun* grey-brown
line 4   *wiers* wires

line 5   *damaskt* damasked, of a mingled red and white
line 8   *reekes* reeks, is emitted
line 11   *graunt* grant
line 13   *(I think) my love as rare* my beloved as beautiful
line 14   *any she* any woman; *beli'd* belied, described in lies; *compare*
              (noun) comparisons (an alternative reading with *she* as the
              subject of *belied* may be possible)

c) Shakespeare's 'Sonnet 130' is often referred to as an 'anti-Petrarchan sonnet'. Can you guess why? Make sure you understand the parodic point of Shakespeare's poem: does he criticize and ridicule his mistress, the Dark Lady, who differs so much from the Petrarchan ideal of 'fair' female beauty? In fact, this sonnet is anti-Petrarchan in some sense and 'very Petrarchan' in another sense. Can you figure out why?

DISCUSSION

These three poems share their overall theme (the praise of the poet's mistress and, more precisely, the praise of her physical beauty) but they have little else in common.

a) Spenser's sonnet sounds rather artificial because most lines are built up on the basis of a recurrent syntactic pattern: her + part of the body + like + name of flower. The entire sonnet seems to contain but one idea: Spenser's mistress smells better than flowers. Yet the poem has some saving graces; the exotic names of flowers provide it with some strange allure and, if you read the poem aloud, you will notice that it possesses a certain sweet melody: the abundance of iambic pentameters together with the high rate of *alliteration* gives the sonnet a pleasing musicality, **alliteration** like variations on a theme. Some may think, however, that this is not enough to make them enjoy this sonnet: the technique of fragmentation employed by the poet seems to dehumanize the mistress; she is not seen as a rational human being but rather as an aesthetic object – or as a collection of static objects.

b) Watson's poem may have been considered by some of his contemporaries to be a sonnet, but it would probably not be seen as a sonnet today. It has, however, much in common with the sonnet form: the rhyme pattern resembles the structure of the sestet of the English sonnet (a quatrain plus a couplet) and the last couplet in the poem, which provides the turning point for the poem, also functions like the final couplet in a sonnet. However, Watson's poem is eighteen, not fourteen lines long. In fact, one could almost say that it is a mini-sequence of shortened sonnets: three miniature sonnets in a row.

    With regard to its content, the poem offers an orthodox description of a Petrarchan mistress, whose face responds to a well-established canon of beauty: blond hair, bright eyes, white forehead and neck, straight nose, rosy cheeks, red lips and sweet-smelling breath. The form of the poem is also predictably within the parameters of Petrarchan rhetoric: the poem consists of a series of comparisons in which the mistress's facial features are seen to surpass the beauty of gold and the stars, roses and lilies, coral and swans. Watson's poem relies, like Spenser's, on the repetition of a syntactic structure which again begins with 'her + part of the body'. However, the effect is very different: there is none of the musicality of Spenser's poem and the comparisons sound mechanical and unexciting. Part of the difference lies in the novelty of Spenser's comparisons (comparing a woman's nipples with young jasmine which has just blossomed is more ingenious than comparing a woman's lips with coral stone, as Watson does) but the difference is also due to the successful use made of 'sound effects' (metre and alliteration) in Spenser's poem.

However, Watson offers, at least, an amusing turn at the end. Whether it was intended or not, the last couplet offers the chance to construct an ironic reading of the poem: after having nagged about his mistress's beauty for fifteen lines, suddenly the poet claims that her beauty leaves him speechless ('Her vertues all so great as make me mute') and he feels the need to reassure the reader that now he has finished with her face he does not intend to continue with the rest of her body ('What other partes she hath I neede not say,/ Whose face alone is cause of my decaye').

anti-Petrarchan

c) Shakespeare's Sonnet 130 is considered *anti-Petrarchan* because the poet uses its first ten lines to deny his mistress the attributes of Petrarchan beauty. In fact, the anti-Petrarchism consists in reversing the Petrarchan rhetorical technique of comparing items in the mistress's face to the sun, coral, snow, roses, etc. Instead of saying that the mistress's eyes, lips, breasts and cheeks surpass these natural beauties, as in the Watson or Spenser poems, Shakespeare denies that the former come victorious out of the comparison. However, the poet never says his mistress is ugly or devoid of beauty: the entire poem becomes a parody of Petrarchan conventions when we reach the final couplet. The poet now makes clear that he thinks Petrarchan rhetorical conventions are false, so

hyperbole

he will not use *hyperbolic* comparisons to praise his mistress's beauty. Yet – we learn only now – the poet thinks after all that his mistress is as beautiful as any other mistress who is compared to the sun, coral, snow or roses. So, immediately after turning upside-down the conventional comparisons used by Petrarchan poets, Shakespeare turns out to be thoroughly Petrarchan in the sonnet's final defiant statement of his mistress's beauty.

A sonnet is generally thought of as a love poem. It is true that the amount of love sonnets produced in Italy before the sonnet form reached England and the influence of Petrarch's own sonnets may justify this association between sonnet and love poem. This is, however, a slightly distorted image of the sonnet: as the sonnets you have so far read in this chapter show, the English sonnet started life as a protean form which could be used as a vehicle to discuss many issues besides love. Surrey used the sonnet to reflect on topics such as death, courage and friendship. Shakespeare's sonnets deal with topics which are as varied as the advantages of marriage, nobility, children's education, poetry, painting, cosmetics, the flow of time, or rivalry amongst writers. His sonnets also include a satire of contemporary mores, as in the following one:

LOOKING INTO THE ORNAMENTED CASE: SONNETS AND THEIR SUBJECT-MATTER

William Shakespeare, *Sonnet* 66

Tyr'd with all these for restfull death I cry:
As to behold desert a begger borne,
And needie nothing trimd in jollitie,
And purest faith unhappily forsworne,
And gilded honor shamefully misplast,
And maiden vertue rudely strumpeted,
And right perfection wrongfully disgrac'd,
And strength by limping sway disablèd,
And arte made tung-tide by authoritie,
And Folly (Doctor-like) controuling skill,
And simple Truth miscalde Simplicitie,
And captive good attending Captaine ill.
Tyr'd with all these, from these would I be gone,
Save that to dye, I leave my love alone.

GLOSSARY

line 1   *Tyr'd* tired
line 2   *desert* merit, worth; *a begger borne* born as a beggar
line 3   *needie* needy; *trimd* trimmed
line 5   *misplast* misplaced
line 9   *arte made tung-tide* art made tongue-tied
line 10 *controuling* controlling
line 11 *miscalde* miscalled
line 14 *dye* die

In fact, sometimes, if one looks closely into the miniature, one may discover that the love topic is only one – and sometimes not the most important – of the many topics addressed in a single English Renaissance sonnet.

The diversity of topics which can be dealt with in a sonnet is one of the obstacles which may hinder our grasping the meanings of these poems: reading an Elizabethan sonnet can sometimes be compared to separating several threads which have got – beautifully – entangled. This is the case in the sonnets which both Philip Sidney (1554–86) and Edmund Spenser placed at the opening of their respective sonnet-sequences. Both these sequences, Sidney's *Astrophil and Stella* (written 1580–4; published 1591) and Spenser's *Amoretti* may have been written for contemporary ladies: Sidney may – or may not – have written his sequence for Penelope Devereux and Spenser may have written it for his future wife Elizabeth Boyle. Regardless of their real addressee, the fact is that the poems in these sequences are addressed by a poet to a lady with whom the poet professes to be in love. However, the initial sonnet in both sequences is not merely – and in one of them not even mostly – about love.

Sir Philip Sidney, *Astrophil and Stella*, Sonnet 1

Loving in truth, and faine in verse my love to show,
That she (deare she) might take some pleasure of my paine:
Pleasure might cause her reade, reading might make her know,
Knowledge might pitie winne, and pitie grace obtaine.
I sought fit wordes, to paint the blackest face of woe,
Studying inventions fine, her wittes to entertaine,
Oft turning others leaves, to see if thence would flow,
Some fresh and fruitfull showers, upon my sunne-burn'd braine.
But wordes came halting forth, wanting Inventions stay,
Invention Natures child, fledde step-dame Studies blowes:
And others feete, still seem'd but strangers in my way,
Thus great with child to speake, and helplesse in my throwes,
Biting my trewand pen, beating my selfe for spite:
Foole, saide my Muse to me, looke in thy heart and write.

GLOSSARY

line 1   *faine* fain, willing
line 2   *paine* pain
line 4   *pitie* pity; *winne* win; *obtaine* obtain
line 5   *wordes* words
line 6   *Studying inventions fine* trying to decide on suitable topics for his sonnets; *wittes* wits; *entertaine* entertain, amuse
line 7   *others leaves* other people's pages, writings
line 8   *sunne-burn'd* sun-burnt; *braine* brain
line 9   *wanting Inventions stay* lacking the power to settle on a topic
line 10 *fledde . . . blowes* fled with light, ladylike steps from the blows of Study (when you are trying to decide what to write about, too much study can kill invention or imagination, because imagination is Nature's child and therefore not easily subjected to rules)
line 11 *others feete* others' (metrical) feet; *seem'd* seemed

line 12 *great with child* the poet is metaphorically pregnant and wants to give birth to his ideas in his poem; *throwes* throws, pangs of pain
line 13 *trewand* truant, lazy

Edmund Spenser, *Amoretti*, Sonnet 1

Happy ye leaues when as those lilly hands,
which hold my life in their dead doing might
shall handle you and hold in loues soft bands,
lyke captiues trembling at the victors sight.
And happy lines, on which with starry light,
those lamping eyes will deigne sometimes to look
and read the sorrowes of my dying spright,
written with teares in harts close bleeding book.
And happy rymes bath'd in the sacred brooke,
of Helicon whence she deriued is,
when ye behold that Angels blessed looke,
my soules long lacked foode, my heauens blis.
Leaues, lines, and rymes, seeke her to please alone,
whom if ye please, I care for other none.

GLOSSARY

line 1 *ye leaues* you leaves, sheets of paper
line 2 *dead doing might* death-causing power (the lady has the power to kill the poet if she does not approve of his poems)
line 3 *loues* Love's
line 4 *lyke captiues* like captives; *victors* victor's
line 6 *lamping* shining, resplendent
line 7 *spright* courage, vitality, vigour
line 8 *in harts* in the heart's
line 9 *rymes* rhymes; *bath'd* bathed; *brooke* brook, small stream
line 10 *Helicon* mountain in Greece thought to be the home of the Muses, the nine Greek goddesses who support literature, music and the fine arts; *deriued* derived
line 12 *my soules* my soul's; *foode* food; *my heauens blis* my heaven's bliss
line 13 *seeke* seek

a) Try to separate – underlining would help – the lines in each sonnet in which the poet speaks of love and those in which he speaks of something else. See if you can make any sense of those other lines: which topics do they introduce, which relations exist between them? You could jot down ideas in two separate lists, one for each sonnet.

b) Now that you have made a list of the non-amorous topics in each sonnet, see which ones are shared by both sonnets and which ones are not. If you are working with other students, you could compare notes and discuss cases in which there is disagreement.

DISCUSSION

a) Spenser's sonnet clearly states the poet's love for the lady only when we reach the final couplet: 'I care for other none' (l. 14). It is true, however, that he has sprinkled his sonnet with Petrarchan *topoi*, so it is clear, right from the first lines, that love is one of the topics present in this poem: 'those lilly hands,/ which hold my life in their dead doing might' (ll. 1–2), 'loues soft bands' (l. 3), 'lyke captiues trembling at the victors sight' (l. 4), 'starry light' (l. 5), 'those lamping eyes will deigne sometimes to look' (l. 6), 'the sorrowes of my dying spright' (l. 7), 'teares in harts close bleeding book' (l. 8), 'that Angels blessed looke' (l. 11), 'my soules long lacked foode, my heauens blis' (l. 12). In fact, this sonnet can be read as a sampler of *amour courtois* or a brief guide to Petrarchism: the lady's beauty is idealized and conventionally described, love is equated with suffering, the lover is depicted as love's prisoner and happiness is only attainable if the lady takes notice of the lover's efforts to please her. Despite all this, love is not the only topic of the poem: the poem is not addressed to the lady, to Cupid or to a fellow sufferer, but to the poet's own poetry. The poet, in fact, addresses – by means of the rhetorical figure of *apostrophe* – the pages ('leaues') on which his poems are written, the lines which give shape to his thoughts and the rhymes which bind these thoughts together, so the sonnet becomes a conversation the poet holds with his own sonnet-sequence.

amour courtois

apostrophe

In Sidney's sonnet, love enjoys an even less central place; references to Petrarchan love cluster around each other almost exclusively in the first quatrain: 'Loving in truth' (l. 1), 'faine . . . my love to show' (l. 1), 'deare she' (l. 2), 'my paine' (l. 2), 'Pleasure . . . grace obtaine' (ll. 3–4). In the second and third quatrains, as in the final couplet, mentions of love, the lady or the condition of the Petrarchan lover are scarce; there are only some echoes of the first quatrain in 'the blackest face of woe' (l. 5), 'her wittes to entertaine' (l. 6), and 'looke in thy heart' (l. 14), which respectively recall 'my paine' (l. 2), 'pleasure might cause her reade' (l. 3) and 'Loving in truth' (l. 1). Note, however, that 'helplesse in my throwes' (l. 12) does not refer to the suffering condition of the Petrarchan lover, but to the pain which accompanies literary creation. As a matter of fact, most of the poem deals with topics associated with literary activity, with reading and writing; it offers a self-portrait of Sidney writing his own sonnet-sequence and discusses the many difficulties a writer has to face: the selection of one's topic (*inventio*), the search for ideas in other people's writings, the struggle with words, the elusive nature of inspiration, the need to master technical matters, the role of fact and fiction in literature, and the pain, the suffering, the biting of one's pen, all of which lead to self-contempt. There is an allusion to reading already in the first quatrain, 'Pleasure might cause her reade, reading might make her know' (l. 3), but most of the topics dealing with reading and writing are more fully elaborated from line 5 to line 14: 'I sought fit wordes' (l. 5), 'Studying inventions fine' (l. 6), 'Oft turning others leaves, to see if thence would flow,/ Some fresh and fruitfull showers, upon my sunne-burn'd braine' (ll. 7–8), 'But wordes came halting forth' (l. 9), 'Invention . . . fledde' (l. 10), 'others feete . . . strangers in my way' (l. 11), 'great with child to speake' (l. 12), 'helplesse in my throwes' (l. 12), 'Biting my trewand pen' (l. 13), 'beating my selfe for spite' (l. 13), 'looke in thy heart and write' (l. 14).

b) Both sonnets rest on the idea that poetry springs from a desire to please the loved one; both show an image of the poet as a being who loves and suffers; both assume that the narration of the poet's sorrow will entertain and give pleasure to their respective ladies. Both depict the act of creation as painful: 'written with teares' (Spenser, l. 8) and 'helplesse in my throwes' (Sidney, l. 12). But here similitude ends. Whereas Spenser depicts poetry statically as a finished product, Sidney presents poetry dynamically as a process. Spenser clearly acknowledges that the end of writing is to please his lady – and he does not care if others do not think highly of the poems which make up the sonnet-sequence. For Spenser, love is the reason why one writes. Sidney, instead, is more deeply concerned with issues relating to creative writing: his sonnet is a much more sophisticated elaboration on the steps, the methods, the decisions, the difficulties which surround the act of literary creation. Sidney's initial sonnet dedicates more room to the difficulties found in producing imaginative literature and writing poetry than to the discussion of his love for Stella: the real difficulties of the Petrarchan lover who wants to show his love in verse are found in grappling with form (metrical feet are strangers), in the relation between invention and nature, fact and fiction (look inside your heart before you write), in the problem of originality (should one look into other people's work in search of inspiration?), in the familiar picture of the writer struggling to give shape to thoughts (biting one's pen). In Sidney's poem, it is the 'braine' and not the heart that is 'burn'd', and the last word in the sonnet is 'write' not 'love'. For Sidney, love is an excuse to write.

FROM THE ELIZABETHAN SONNET TO THE PRESENT

Post-Renaissance poets have often subverted the traditional sonnet structure in order to achieve particular effects: see e.g. Milton's 'When I Consider' and Wordsworth's 'The World Is Too Much With Us' for good examples of this (both poems are reproduced and discussed in the next chapter). Elizabeth Barrett Browning (1806–61), a Victorian poet, took up again the fashion of the sonnet-sequence in *Sonnets from the Portuguese* and, interestingly, she exchanges the roles of lover and loved one: in some of her sonnets, the poet writes as the loved one, not the lover. A twentieth-century

American poet who subverts not the formal or structural expectations but the thematic conventions of the sonnet genre is Edna St Vincent Millay (1892–1950). See if you can spot how the following sonnet (published in 1923) undermines the masculine assumptions about women and love which are typical of the sonnet genre:

Edna St Vincent Millay

Oh, oh, you will be sorry for that word!
Give back my book and take my kiss instead.
Was it my enemy or my friend I heard,
"What a big book for such a little head!"
Come, I will show you now my newest hat,
And you may watch me purse my mouth and prink!
Oh, I shall love you still, and all of that.
I never again shall tell you what I think.
I shall be sweet and crafty, soft and sly;
You will not catch me reading any more:
I shall be called a wife to pattern by;
And some day when you knock and push the door,
Some sane day, not too bright and not too stormy,
I shall be gone, and you may whistle for me.

RE-READING THE SONNET

Now that you have admired the picture nestling inside, you can close the miniature and enjoy its outward case again: the beautiful exterior will remind you of the beautiful content it preserves. The sonnet is an idea, or a collection of ideas, cased in a jewel-like shape. Much of the pleasure of reading sonnets is derived from 're-reading' them: each time one opens and closes the case, one sees things one did not see before. And by looking at the miniature and its case repeatedly one can more easily enjoy the fusion of both arts: the jeweller's and the painter's. Like the miniature, a good sonnet is the product of a good craftsman and a good artist and, like the works of each of them, it has to be examined many times before we can really appreciate its value.

ACTIVITY: (RE)WRITING THE ELIZABETHAN SONNET

a) **Rewrite one of the sonnets discussed in this chapter: e.g. rewrite Wyatt's sonnet from the point of view of Anne Boleyn, stating, for example, her right to choose whom she pleases, or her love for Wyatt but her fear of upsetting Henry VIII's tyrannical nature. Or rewrite Surrey's elegiac sonnet and experiment with the gender and social identity of addresser and addressee: from a female poet to a female friend, or from a female poet to her father, for example. You could also write a sonnet as an answer to Drayton's sonnet quoted above, in which he asks his lady to make it up with him.**

b) **Alternatively, you could write an entirely new sonnet about somebody you love, either following the traditional sonnet structure (the Italian or the English) and the Petrarchan conventions associated with the genre or disrupting some of these poetic *topoi*.**

PROJECT WORK: THE ROMANTIC SONNET

After suffering a displacement during the Restoration and the eighteenth century, when other poetic forms were more popular, the sonnet again became a favourite form with poets during the Romantic period. Make your own personal collection of sonnets written by Romantic poets such as Wordsworth, Coleridge, Shelley and Keats, and if you can, include in your anthology some poems by less canonical poets such as Cowper, or women poets such as Anna Seward (1747–1809), Charlotte Smith (1749–1806) and Helen Maria Williams (1762–1827). You can then arrange your poems according to formal aspects such as type of sonnet, structure, rhyme patterns, etc. and/or according to topics addressed by the poet. You could also explore alternative criteria of classification: according to dialogic/non-dialogic nature of the sonnet, according to the gender of addresser or addressee. Finally, prepare a brief essay on the Romantic sonnet, taking the present chapter as a guide. (Before you get started read Chapter 2 of this book, which will introduce you to some aspects of Romantic poetry and also includes sonnets by Wordsworth and Shelley.)

PROJECT WORK: THE DIALOGIC SONNET

Many sonnets take the form of a sort of confession the poet makes, so they simply offer the 'voice' of the poet addressing the reader or a third party (a lover, a friend, a patron). An example is the sonnet by Wyatt discussed in this chapter, in which the poet addresses would-be lovers of Anne Boleyn. However, there are sonnets which possess a dialogic structure, sonnets which have a built-in dialogue, such as the sonnet by Barnfield on p. 12. These dialogic sonnets have one clear asset: they can show the different points of view of the 'voices' involved in the dialogue. You could build up a small anthology of sonnets which possess this kind of 'interactive' nature (you already have a few in this chapter) and study who the participants in the dialogue are, what power relations obtain between them, how the poet goes about the problem of identifying each voice, how the antithetical structure of the sonnet is exploited to present conflicting ideas expressed by various voices, etc. An easy one to start your anthology with is the sonnet jointly constructed by Shakespeare's Romeo and Juliet during Capulet's feast (*Romeo and Juliet*, Act I, Scene v), but there are many others: the opening sonnet of *Astrophil and Stella* gives a voice to both Astrophil and his Muse, and there is also Spenser's sonnet 75 in *Amoretti*, which gives a voice to the poet's mistress. You can enlarge your collection with sonnets from other periods, and a twentieth-century sonnet you might consider using is W.H. Auden's 'From reader to rider'.

REFERENCES
AND
SUGGESTIONS
FOR FURTHER
READING

Elizabethan sonnets appear in many poetry anthologies. One which is particularly useful is *The Penguin Book of Renaissance Verse 1509–1659*, ed. David Norbrook and H.R. Woudhuysen (Penguin, 1992). This anthology contains many sonnets alongside other Elizabethan poems, as well as an excellent introduction. The poems are arranged by topic, so the reader can see how sonnets share ideas and themes with other poems. A useful modern guide to poetry is Tom Furniss and Michael Bath's *Reading Poetry* (Prentice Hall, 1996), which includes a section on the sonnet. Gary Waller's *English Poetry of the Sixteenth Century* (Longman, 1993), published in the Longman Literature in English series, is a very good survey of poetry written in the period and it has two interesting chapters on the Sidney Circle and Lady Mary Wroth. More specifically on the sonnet, a valuable introduction, mostly for issues concerning the sonnet as poetic form, is John Fuller's *The Sonnet* in The Critical Idiom series (Methuen, 1972). A classic discussion of the Elizabethan sonnet can be found in J.W. Lever, *The Elizabethan Love Sonnet* (Methuen, 1956). Michael Spiller's *The Development of the Sonnet* (Routledge, 1992) is very informative and should be consulted. The comparison between the sonnet and the miniature owes much to a seminal article by Patricia Fumerton, '"Secret" Arts: Elizabethan Miniatures and Sonnets', in *Representing the Renaissance*, ed. Stephen Greenblatt (University of California Press, 1988: 93–133). This article includes reproductions of several Elizabethan miniatures, including Hilliard's *Man Against a Background of Flames*.

2
WHAT'S SYNTAX GOT TO DO WITH POETRY?
On Puritan Mind-Style and Romantic World-View

Graham Greene's novel *A Gun For Sale* (1936) opens as follows:

[1] Murder didn't mean much to Raven. It was just a new job. You had to be careful. You had to use your brains. It was not a question of hatred.

Greene here uses a sequence of *simple sentences* (sentences of only one clause), giving the impression of a highly syncopated style. He chose not to use a more *complex sentence* structure in which, for example, the different sentences would be linked together by means of coordinating conjunctions such as *and*, *for*, *but*. This would have resulted in a sentence of the following type:

simple sentence

complex sentence

[2] Murder didn't mean much to Raven, for it was just a new job: you had to be careful and you had to use your brains, but it was not a question of hatred.

In the case of *coordination* (sentence 2), all the clauses are of equal syntactic status. However, it would also have been possible to *subordinate* the clauses to one main clause:

coordination

subordination

[3] Murder didn't mean much to Raven, because it was just a new job in which you had to be careful and to use your brains, though it was not a question of hatred.

The dependent clauses in sentence 3 are introduced by subordinating conjunctions (*because*, *though*) or they are relative clauses dependent on the noun phrase *a new job*. Sentence 3 with the main clause placed at the beginning and followed by a number of dependent clauses is said to have a *loose* sentence structure. If, on the other hand, the dependent clauses are put first and the main clause is left until the very end, the sentence is said to have a *periodic* or *suspensive* sentence structure:

loose structure

periodic/ suspensive structure

[4] Because it was just a new job in which you had to be careful and to use your brains (though it was not a question of hatred), murder didn't mean much to Raven.

Here completion of the message is delayed until we reach the sentence-final main clause. In this way, periodic syntax is a highly effective rhetorical and dramatic technique of leading up to a climax. It builds up suspense in the reader, since the main-clause information is – at least temporarily – withheld.

This gives us the following network of syntactic choices which, though it simplifies the options made available by the English language, is sufficient for our purposes:

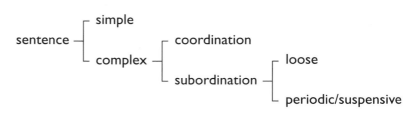

mind-style

Our argument in this chapter will be to show that choices from this system of syntactic patterns – whether simple or complex, coordinate or subordinate, loose or periodic – refract (in the sense of both reflecting and creating) a particular *mind-style*, a particular way of conceiving of the world. And consequently, as we shall see later on in the chapter when we look at a poem by Milton, any systematic changes in the choices of syntactic patterns would be indicative of a development in the world-view of the person who made them.

But for the moment, we would like you to look again at text (1) above and compare its effects with 2, 3 and 4. **To what extent does Greene's choice of simple sentences refract the typical ways of thinking of Raven, the professional killer of *A Gun For Sale?***

Next, compare the beginning of Greene's novel with the openings of three other novels reproduced below and study the sentence structure (simple or complex, coordinate or subordinate, loose or periodic) of each extract.

[5] William Faulkner's *The Sound and the Fury* (1931) (Benji, the mentally retarded narrator, is watching some people playing golf):

Through the fence, between the curling flower spaces, I could see them hitting. They were coming toward where the flag was and I went along the fence. Luster was hunting in the grass by the flower tree. They took the flag out, and they were hitting. Then they put the flag back and they went to the table, and he hit and the other hit. Then they went on, and I went along the fence. Luster came away from the flower tree and we went along the fence and they stopped and we stopped and I looked through the fence while Luster was hunting in the grass.

[6] Laurence Sterne's *Tristram Shandy* (1781):

I wish either my father or my mother, or indeed both of them, as they were in duty both equally bound to it, had minded what they were about when they begot me; had they duly consider'd how much depended upon what they were then doing; – that not only the production of a rational Being was concerned in it, but that possibly the happy formation and temperature of his body, perhaps his genius and the very cast of his mind; – and, for aught they knew to the contrary, even the fortunes of his whole house might take their turn from the humours and dispositions which were then uppermost; – Had they duly weighed and considered all this, and proceeded accordingly, – I am verily persuaded I should have made a quite different figure in the world from that in which the reader is likely to see me.

[7] Kazuo Ishiguro's *The Remains of the Day* (1989):

It seems increasingly likely that I really will undertake the expedition that has been preoccupying my imagination now for some days. An expedition, I should say, which I will undertake alone, in the comfort of Mr Farraday's Ford; an expedition which, as I foresee it, will take me through much of the finest countryside of England to the West Country, and may keep me away from Darlington Hall for as much as five or six days. The idea of such a journey came about, I should point out, from a most kind suggestion put to me by Mr Farraday himself one afternoon almost a fortnight ago, when I had been dusting the portraits in the library.

Do the various styles help you to construct a mental image of what the protagonists – respectively, Faulkner's Benji, Sterne's Tristram and Ishiguro's butler – are like?

DISCUSSION NOTES

extract 5: the sentence structure is predominantly coordinate, with *and* being used far too frequently (which gives a rather 'childlike' feel to the passage)
extract 6: predominantly periodic sentence structure
extract 7: predominantly loose sentence structure

In the remainder of this chapter, we turn to poetry and illustrate how poets achieve certain effects through an idiosyncratic use of syntactic options.

MILTON'S 'WHEN   Milton's sonnet was probably written in 1651–2, just as Milton had
I CONSIDER'   become completely blind. In it, he wonders how God can expect him
to work for Him now that he is reduced to a state of physical darkness.
How can he continue writing both poetry and political pamphlets,
or indeed continue working as Cromwell's Secretary for Foreign
Tongues? The Puritan Commonwealth had been established in 1649
under Cromwell as Lord Protector, and King Charles I had been
executed. Milton had taken an active part in these momentous events
by writing pamphlets against the monarch, against the episcopal
system of Church government, for divorce and for the freedom of the
press. But his future as both poet and politician was now endangered
by his blindness. In his sonnet, Milton expressed his reaction to this
terrible calamity. He left the poem untitled, but in anthologies it is
usually referred to either as 'When I Consider' or 'On His Blindness'.

When I consider how my light is spent,
Ere half my days, in this dark world and wide,
And that one talent which is death to hide
Lodged with me useless, though my soul more bent
To serve therewith my maker, and present
My true account, lest he returning chide,
Doth God exact day-labour, light denied,
I fondly ask; but Patience, to prevent
That murmur, soon replies, God doth not need
Either man's work or his own gifts; who best
Bear his mild yoke, they serve him best; his state
Is kingly. Thousands at his bidding speed
And post o'er land and ocean without rest:
They also serve who only stand and wait.

a) **Study the form of the poem. Is it a Petrarchan or a Shakespearean sonnet? What
is the rhyme-scheme? Are the traditional sonnet divisions respected?**
b) **Study the sentence structure of the octave in terms of the categories introduced
above (simple or complex, coordinate or subordinate, loose or periodic). In
what ways does the sentence structure enact the poet's state of mind?**
c) **Finally, consider how both the sentence structure and the poet's state of mind
change in the sestet.**

DISCUSSION   a) The rhyme-scheme of Milton's poem is typical of Petrarchan
sonnets, but the traditional structure is somewhat disrupted by
enjambement   the many *enjambements* or run-on lines, including lines which
overrun the boundaries of the quatrains (ll. 4, 8) and tercets (l.
11). Moreover, the main break in the Petrarchan sonnet, which is
the break between octave and sestet, occurs here already in the
middle of line 8. Before reading on, think about the effect of this
disruption of the traditional sonnet form.

b) The sentence structure in the octave is periodic, with many dependent (or subordinate) clauses leading up to the main clause in line 8 ('I fondly ask'). In fact, the syntax is so complex that different readers have come up with different grammatical readings. We have no space here to go into alternative readings, so we just present one possible way of making sense of this sentence and would ask you to compare it with your own grammatical reading:

When I consider how my light is spent . . .
and (how) that one talent . . . (is) lodged with me useless,
though my soul (is) more bent to serve . . . and (to) present . . . ,
I fondly ask: 'Doth God exact day-labour, (although) light (is)
    denied?'

Bracketed words are words that have been introduced to complete, and make sense of, the grammatical construction.

The second part of our question here ('In what ways does the sentence structure enact the poet's state of mind?') is somewhat misleading in that it might suggest that syntax creates meaning. This is patently absurd, since it is always readers who produce meaning. But the point that we are making is that, when readers try to understand Milton's sentence, they may find its syntactic intricacies extremely difficult to process. They may experience confusion, as they attempt to sort through the complex grammatical structure of the sentence (what we have tried to do above). They may also experience a confusion of voices, wondering initially whether in line 7 they hear the voice of God who returns chiding, and only realizing as they read on that line 7 is in fact still the voice of the poet questioning God's justice. Readers might therefore attribute all this confusion that they experience during processing to the poet's state of mind when he was writing the poem. In other words, Milton's syntax would be an *experiential syntax*, which **experiential** contributes to our perception of his state of mind as full of **syntax** confusion, agitation, anguish and intense emotion. The grammatical 'confusion' is an appropriate form in which to express the mental confusion of a person rebelling against God and doubting His justice.

The poet's protest and complaint builds up to the almost blasphemous question of line 7, in which the voice of impatience, itself a sign of not only physical but also spiritual darkness, is speaking through the poet. But the poet immediately realizes that he is being presumptuous and guilty of the sin of pride (hybris), and so in the main clause of line 8 ('I fondly ask') he inserts an adverb ('fondly') which clearly shows that he disaffiliates and distances himself from the position expressed in lines 1–7.

c) The sestet presents the reply given by the inner voice of patience. The main clause occurs at the very beginning ('but

Patience . . . soon replies'), and is followed by a series of independent clauses with six further main verbs (doth not need, serve, is, speed, post, serve). This sentence structure, which is far less complex than in the octave, suggests a change of mind in the poet, a resolution of his inner conflict, as he regains his calm, confidence and inner peace. The metre, too, becomes regular towards the end, with line 14 being not only a complete syntactic unit but also a perfectly formed iambic pentameter.

Puritanism

Throughout our analysis, we have referred to the speaker as 'the poet' or 'Milton', since we have chosen to read the poem as autobiographical. We see it as a fascinating and terrifying account of a seventeenth-century *Puritan* mind undergoing and eventually resolving an inner conflict. After an initial fear that he might no longer be one of God's elect (according to the Puritan doctrine of predestination), the poet ends by seeing himself again as God's poet, serving God both by the passive acceptance of His will ('his mild yoke') and by a more active attitude of resisting all evil. These two attitudes are epitomized by the verb 'stand' (line 14), which Milton often uses — also in his long epic poem *Paradise Lost* — not only in the passive sense but also in the more active sense of 'withstanding'.

PROJECT WORK: PURITANISM

Seventeenth-century economic and political problems favoured the rise of Puritanism, which culminated in the beheading of King Charles I and the establishment of the Puritan Commonwealth (1649–1660). Puritanism was a movement full of contradictions: its work ethic was combined with a highly repressive morality and zeal for righteousness; its emphasis on the individual conscience and on freedom of thought, as well as its commitment to radical social reforms, was often contradicted in practice by the authoritarian and conservative leanings of some Puritan leaders. Nevertheless, the Puritan ideals had a powerful impact on the literary imagination. Study to what extent a somewhat secularized version of Puritan individualism 'informs' such eighteenth-century works as Daniel Defoe's *Robinson Crusoe* (1719) or *Moll Flanders* (1721).

WORDSWORTH'S 'THE WORLD IS TOO MUCH WITH US'

From the Puritan poet John Milton we move to the Romantic poets, whose concept of God, unlike Milton's, is an impersonal and diffuse one. According to the critic T.E. Hulme, romanticism is 'spilt religion' (1924/1987: 118), relying as it does on the *pantheistic* notion of a divine presence that pervades the whole of nature. Therefore the Romantic poets feel convinced that what gives our life meaning is our ability to respond to the divine presence in nature. William

pantheism

Wordsworth (1770–1850) expresses this conviction for example in the following poem, which we should like you to look at briefly before we turn to 'The World Is Too Much With Us':

My Heart Leaps Up When I Behold

My heart leaps up when I behold
   A rainbow in the sky:
So was it when my life began;
So is it now I am a man;
So be it when I shall grow old,
   Or let me die!
The Child is father of the Man;
And I could wish my days to be
Bound each to each by natural piety.

Can you explain a) what is unusual about the meaning of line 7 and b) what the poet means by 'natural piety' (line 9)?

DISCUSSION NOTES

a) The child is father of the man because the child has the ability to respond to nature and passes it on to the adult. In this way, the adult has to learn from the child, and must try to preserve this intuitive link with nature. But often, in the passage from childhood to adulthood, our intuitive understanding of nature is lost. Something comes between the adult and nature and breaks up the connection, and this something is what Wordsworth refers to as 'the world'.

The World Is Too Much With Us

The world is too much with us; late and soon
Getting and spending, we lay waste our powers:
Little we see in Nature that is ours;
We have given our hearts away, a sordid boon!
This sea that bares her bosom to the moon;
The winds that will be howling at all hours,
And are upgathered now like sleeping flowers;
For this, for everything, we are out of tune;
It moves us not. – Great God! I'd rather be
A Pagan suckled in a creed outworn;
So might I, standing on this pleasant lea,
Have glimpses that would make me less forlorn;
Have sight of Proteus rising from the sea;
Or hear old Triton blow his wreathed horn.

a) Study the form of the poem: is it a Petrarchan or Shakespearean sonnet? What is the rhyme-scheme? Are the sonnet divisions respected or is there a structural irregularity? Is the irregularity the same as in Milton's sonnet?

b) How can we account for this irregularity? Can we link it with the speaker's state of mind, as we did in our analysis of Milton's poem?
c) What are the similarities and/or differences between Wordsworth's religion of nature and the hippie world-view of the 1960s or the Green Party politics of the 1980s and 1990s?

DISCUSSION NOTES

Note that in both Milton's and Wordsworth's sonnets, the break between octave and sestet is irregular, but whereas in Milton it occurs already in the middle of line 8, in Wordsworth it does not occur until the middle of line 9. Whereas Milton's speaker is intent on stifling the inner voice of impatience as quickly as possible, Wordsworth's speaker gives full expression to his feelings of despair. He ends the poem with an emotional outburst ('Great God!') in which he expresses his disgust at the hollowness and sterility of early nineteenth-century society and proclaims that he would feel 'less forlorn' as an ancient Greek pagan. Please pause for just a moment to consider why Wordsworth finds the ancient Greeks' attitude to nature infinitely preferable to that of his materialistic contemporaries, and also what his reaction might be to our own society's attitude towards nature (this is of course what question c above is getting at).

KEATS' 'TO AUTUMN'

Here is a romantic ode by John Keats (1795–1821), who wrote it at the age of twenty-four:

To Autumn

Season of mists and mellow fruitfulness,
Close bosom-friend of the maturing sun;
Conspiring with him how to load and bless
With fruit the vines that round the thatch-eaves run;
To bend with apples the moss'd cottage-trees,
And fill all fruit with ripeness to the core;
To swell the gourd, and plump the hazel shells
With a sweet kernel; to set budding more,
And still more, later flowers for the bees,
Until they think warm days will never cease,
For Summer has o'er-brimmed their clammy cells.

Who hath not seen thee oft amid thy store?
Sometimes whoever seeks abroad may find
Thee sitting careless on a granary floor,
Thy hair soft-lifted by the winnowing wind;
Or on a half-reap'd furrow sound asleep,
Drows'd with the fume of poppies, while thy hook
Spares the next swath and all its twined flowers:

And sometimes like a gleaner thou dost keep
Steady thy laden head across a brook;
Or by a cyder-press, with patient look,
Thou watchest the last oozings hours by hours.

Where are the songs of Spring? Ay, where are they?
Think not of them, thou hast thy music too, –
While barred clouds bloom the soft-dying day,
And touch the stubble-plains with rosy hue;
Then in a wailful choir the small gnats mourn
Among the river sallows, borne aloft
Or sinking as the light wind lives or dies;
And full-grown lambs loud bleat from hilly bourn;
Hedge-crickets sing; and now with treble soft
The red-breast whistles from a garden-croft;
And gathering swallows twitter in the skies.

a) **Study the sentence structure of the first stanza. In what ways does it contribute to Keats' evocation of the richness and fruitfulness of autumn? Do you notice any other poetic devices that the poet uses to reinforce his theme? How does the sentence structure change in stanzas 2 and 3?**
b) **At the time of writing this poem, Keats was suffering from frequent attacks of ill health. He knew that he had tuberculosis and that he would die of it in the near future. In fact, he died of it two years later, in 1821. Do you notice any awareness of death in the poem? In which stanza is it the strongest?**
c) **Compare the following two statements by influential twentieth-century critics and find evidence in the poem to support either of these views. The first, by Jerome J. McGann, is a comment on the whole 1820 volume of Keats' poetry in which 'To Autumn' was included; the second one is taken from a highly critical discussion of McGann's argument by Jeremy Hawthorn:**

The Lamia volume represented Keats' effort to show his readers how they might, by entering his poetic space, step aside from the conflicts and tensions, which were so marked an aspect of that period. The whole point of Keats' great and (politically) reactionary book was not to enlist poetry in the service of social and political causes – which is what Byron and Shelley were doing – but to dissolve social and political conflicts in the mediations of art and beauty.

(McGann, 1985: 53)

'To Autumn' was written at a time of extreme social unrest, but also at a time of disappointed liberal hopes so far as developments in France were concerned. The restoration of the monarchy in France in 1815 led to a situation in which reactionary forces throughout Europe attempted to claim that it was now 'back to normal', that a terrible experiment had been made, had failed, and that things were now able to return to what they had always been. . . . What Keats says to his readers – and his rulers – is comparable to what Galileo is reputed to have muttered after his forced recantation to the Inquisition: 'And yet it moves.' Being told that things move is what no reactionary authority wants to hear or to think about. Keats knew that things did move, and he knew that understanding this would weaken reaction and strengthen opposition to it. And no poem insists more effectively upon the fundamental and unstoppable fact of change than does 'To Autumn'.

(Hawthorn, 1996: 176, 179)

DISCUSSION NOTES

a) Note how the 'overloaded' loose sentence structure of stanza I enacts the richness of autumn and at the same time presents each process of ripening as originating from the same source: Autumn, together with the sun, conspires how to

- load and bless the vines with fruit
- bend the trees with apples
- fill the fruit with ripeness
- swell the gourd
- plump the hazel shells with a sweet kernel
- set budding more . . . flowers

SHELLEY'S 'SONNET TO ENGLAND IN 1819'

Percy Bysshe Shelley (1792–1822) was perhaps the most revolutionary of the Romantic poets. He was expelled from Oxford University for writing a pamphlet entitled 'The Necessity of Atheism'. In a hotel register in Switzerland, he added the words 'democrat and atheist' after his name – a most shocking thing to do in early nineteenth-century Europe. He left his wife, Harriet Westbrook, and eloped with Mary Godwin, the daughter of the radical thinkers William Godwin and Mary Wollstonecraft. After Harriet's death, Percy and Mary got married, but he was refused custody of his children from his first marriage. Both because of his radical political views and his unconventional personal life, Shelley had been effectively ostracized by English society. And so the Shelleys settled in Italy in 1818, the year in which the first version of Mary Shelley's famous novel *Frankenstein* was published.

England itself was going through difficult years at the time. Freedom and justice were being trodden under foot by an increasingly repressive and corrupt government. For example, in August 1819, a protest meeting of 70,000 working-class men, women and children, peacefully assembled in the fields of Peterloo outside Manchester, was brutally broken up by the cavalry, with nine people killed and hundreds injured. As for the monarchy, there was no hope from that side either. King George III had been declared incurably insane in 1811 (he was to die in 1820). Here is Shelley's bitter reaction to these events:

Sonnet to England in 1819

An old, mad, blind, despised, and dying king –
Princes, the dregs of their dull race, who flow
Through public scorn – mud from a muddy spring, –
Rulers who neither see, nor feel, nor know,
But leechlike to their fainting country cling,
Till they drop, blind in blood, without a blow –
A people starved and stabbed in the untilled field –
An army, which liberticide and prey
Makes as a two-edged sword to all who wield –
Golden and sanguine laws which tempt and slay;
Religion Christless, Godless – a book sealed;
A Senate – Time's worst statute unrepealed –
Are graves, from which a glorious Phantom may
Burst, to illumine our tempestuous day.

Show how the poet exploits syntax to achieve his poetic effects. (Start off by identifying the subject, verb and complement of Shelley's massive sentence.) Also comment on his use of 'may' in line 13.

The subject of the main clause is the whole of lines 1–12, the verb **DISCUSSION** is 'are' and the complement 'graves' (in line 13). What is the effect of this accumulation of subject noun-phrases? (When you think about this question, you could also go back to page 19 and re-read Shakespeare's 'Sonnet 66', in which Shakespeare uses a highly similar technique and achieves a highly similar effect.)

Shelley's use of 'may' in stressed position at the end of line 13 introduces a more hesitant tone suggesting that he had some doubts whether the English would, similarly to the French, engage in a revolution in order to create a better society.

In a final attempt to pull the various strands of this chapter together, **WORDSWORTH** we should like you to look at another poem by William Wordsworth, **ON MILTON** a sonnet entitled 'London, 1802', in which the poet calls on the spirit of Milton to lead England to a moral regeneration.

London, 1802

Milton! thou shouldst be living at this hour:
England hath need of thee: she is a fen
Of stagnant waters: altar, sword, and pen,
Fireside, the heroic wealth of hall and bower,
Have forfeited their ancient English dower
Of inward happiness. We are selfish men;
Oh! raise us up, return to us again;

And give us manners, virtue, freedom, power.
Thy soul was like a Star, and dwelt apart;
Thou hadst a voice whose sound was like the sea:
Pure as the naked heavens, majestic, free,
So didst thou travel on life's common way,
In cheerful godliness; and yet thy heart
The lowliest duties on herself did lay.

What values does Wordsworth associate with Milton in this poem? Does Wordsworth defend the same values here as Shelley does in 'Sonnet to England in 1819'? (There is a hint towards an answer in the final section of this chapter: References and Suggestions for Further Reading.)

PROJECT WORK: THE ROMANTIC WORLD-VIEW

Look again at Wordsworth's, Keats' and Shelley's poems quoted above. Also read some other Romantic poems that you can get hold of. On the basis of all this material, try to decide whether there is a characteristically Romantic world-view. If yes, define as clearly as possible what it consists in; and if no, explain why you find it difficult or even impossible to talk about a unitary or homogeneous Romantic world-view.

ACTIVITY: SHAKESPEARE'S SONNET 29

Like the speaker of Milton's sonnet discussed above, the speaker of this poem also experiences a feeling of despair at the beginning of the poem. He only calms down towards the end of the poem, where the iambic pentameter rhythm becomes perfectly regular at last. Show how Shakespeare's choice of syntactic structures enacts, or contributes to, this movement from despair to happiness.

Sonnet 29

When in disgrace with fortune and men's eyes
I all alone beweep my outcast state,
And trouble deaf Heaven with my bootless cries,
And look upon myself and curse my fate,
Wishing me like to one more rich in hope,
Featured like him, like him with friends possessed,
Desiring this man's art and that man's scope,
With what I most enjoy contented least –
Yet in these thoughts myself almost despising,
Haply I think on thee, and then my state,
Like to the lark at the break of day arising

From sullen earth, sings hymns at Heaven's gate.
For thy sweet love remembered such wealth brings
That then I scorn to change my state with kings.

Should you wish to explore these issues further in the wider context of Milton's poetry, a good starting-point might be John Barrell's *Poetry, Language and Politics* (Manchester University Press, 1988; chapter 2 is a historicist-based study of syntax and gender in Milton's sonnets). An introduction to Puritanism and its impact on the literary imagination is *God's Plot and Man's Stories: Studies in the Fictional Imagination from Milton to Fielding* by Leopold Damrosch Jr. (University of Chicago Press, 1985).

> **REFERENCES AND SUGGESTIONS FOR FURTHER READING**

T.E. Hulme's essay on romanticism appears in his *Speculations* (Routledge 1924/1987). The two comments on 'To Autumn' are taken from, respectively, Jerome J. McGann's *The Beauty of Inflections: Literary Investigations in Historical Method and Theory* (Clarendon Press, 1985) and Jeremy Hawthorn's *Cunning Passages: New Historicism, Cultural Materialism and Marxism in the Contemporary Literary Debate* (Arnold, 1996).

For more on the Romantic world-view, read Aidan Day's lucid *Romanticism* (1996), published in Routledge's New Critical Idiom series. His basic argument is that 'the politically radical aspects of literature of the period would more usefully be described as "late Enlightenment", while the term Romantic may be taken to define, among other things, an essentially conservative tendency of thought'. As for 'London, 1802', he sees it as a prime example of Wordsworth's political conservatism, where 'the homely hearthside virtues of a feudal order of society are eulogized and equated with a condition of inner, private fulfilment' (1996: 138).

3

WOMEN'S POETRY
Same or Different?

As you may already have noticed, when we study literary texts we usually study them not in a vacuum but in relation to other poems, plays, novels or short stories. We sometimes focus on what two or more literary texts have in common and sometimes, instead, pay attention to their differences.

Read the following passages from two poems and try to see if you can detect any similarities between them:

Anne Sexton (1928–74), *Old*

I'm afraid of needles.
I'm tired of rubber sheets and tubes.
I'm tired of faces I don't know
And now I think that death is starting.
. . . .

Sylvia Plath (1932–63), *Tulips*

The tulips are too excitable, it is winter here.
Look how white everything is, how quiet, how snowed in.
I am learning peacefulness, lying by myself quietly
As the light lies on these white walls, this bed, these hands.
I am nobody; I have nothing to do with explosions.
I have given my name and my day-clothes up to the nurses
And my history to the anaesthetist, and my body to surgeons.
. . . .

Sylvia Plath and Anne Sexton are two twentieth-century North-American poets who wrote poetry roughly about the same time. They both committed suicide – in 1963 and 1974 respectively – leaving behind two bodies of poetry which have come to enrich a sizeable corpus of poetry written by women. Both Plath and Sexton had a history of mental disorder, received treatment and were familiar with a world of hospitals, doctors, nurses and needles. This led them to write poems in which they describe such experiences. They sound very much alike when they write about their being in hospital; their poems share the same sad tone of despondency, as if they had been defeated and are giving in. The two poems also share the overwhelming presence of the first-person pronoun 'I'. Now that we have spotted these similarities we could go on and attribute the tone of the poems to the poets' contact with contemporary practices of psychiatric medicine and the use of 'I' to their being linked to a poetic **confessional** movement called *confessional poetry*. We could then explore the **poetry** relation which these poems in particular and the poetry of Plath and Sexton in general have with other 'confessional poets' or with other literary portraits of women who have been deemed to be in need of psychiatric treatment (see chapter 9 in this Workbook on Jean Rhys' novel *Wide Sargasso Sea*).

We could also read these poems as instances of 'women's poetry', as poems which share some sort of quality because they were written by women who underwent similar experiences. In this sense, 'women's poetry' is seen as a window through which we can observe and study what happens to women, what women think and feel. The study of women's poetry is then no longer simply a part of literary studies but becomes part of a larger discipline: women's studies.

Poetry written by women can thus be studied also from this angle, from a concern with the condition of women as women. If we were to read and analyse a large number of poems written by women across the centuries we could see how there are themes and issues which **female friendship** have repeatedly concerned and interested many women poets. *Female friendship*, the relationship between one woman and another, is one of them. A seventeenth-century poet, Æmilia Lanyer (1569–1645), discusses the relation of friendship and patronage which existed between herself and the Countess of Clifford in a poem entitled 'The Description of Cookham'. Katherine Philips, also a seventeenth-century poet (1632–64), wrote several poems, such as 'To my Excellent Lucasia, on Our Friendship' and 'Friendship's Mystery. To my Dearest Lucasia', in which she shows her concern for another woman. These poems, unlike those by Plath and Sexton, are written in a jubilant tone which celebrates Philips' relationship with her friend and lover Anne Owen, whom she calls 'Lucasia', as in the initial stanza of the second of these poems:

Come, my Lucasia, since we see
That miracles men's faith do move,
By wonder and by prodigy
To the dull angry world let's prove
There's a religion in our love.

Another woman poet, Christina Rossetti (1830–94), has studied the friendship and love which leads one woman to put her life at risk to save the life of another woman in *Goblin Market*, her most celebrated poem. The poem is also a song in praise of sisterhood. The two sisters in the poem, Lizzie and Laura, are so fond of each other that when one of them becomes the victim of the goblin men, the other bravely defies them in order to buy her the fruit she needs. By resisting the goblin men's attempts to make her eat fruit, she obtains the antidote for her sister.

Goblin Market is also an unusual poem in its lively rhythm, its words full of flavour, as in the description Laura gives of all the different types of fruit she has eaten. This is better appreciated when the poem is read aloud. Give it a try when you are alone.

from *Goblin Market*

Morning and evening
Maids heard the goblins cry:
'Come buy our orchard fruits,
Come buy, come buy:
Apples and quinces,
Lemons and oranges,
Plump unpecked cherries,
Melons and raspberries,
Bloom-down-cheeked peaches,
Swart-headed mulberries,
Wild free-born cranberries,
crab-apples, dewberries,
Pine-apples, blackberries,
Apricots, strawberries; –
All ripe together
In summer weather, –
Morns that pass by,
Fair eves that fly;
Come buy, come buy:
Our grapes fresh from the vine,
Pomegranates full and fine,
Dates and sharp bullaces,
Rare pears and greengages,
Damsons and bilberries,
Taste them and try:
Currants and gooseberries,
Bright-fire-like barberries,
Figs to fill your mouth,
Citrons from the South,
Sweet to tongue and sound to eye;
Come buy, come buy.'

Evening by evening
Among the brookside rushes,

Laura bowed her head to hear,
Lizzie veiled her blushes:
Crouching close together
In the cooling weather,
With clasping arms and cautioning lips,
With tingling cheeks and finger tips.
'Lie close,' Laura said,
Pricking up her golden head:
'We must not look at goblin men,
We must not buy their fruits:
Who knows upon what soil they fed
Their hungry thirsty roots?'
. . . .
Laura stretched her gleaming neck
Like a rush-imbedded swan,
Like a lily from the beck,
Like a moonlit poplar branch,
Like a vessel at the launch
When its last restraint is gone.

. . . .
But sweet-tooth Laura spoke in haste:
'Good folk, I have no coin;
To take were to purloin:
I have no copper in my purse,
I have no silver either,
And all my gold is on the furze
That shakes in windy weather
Above the rusty heather.'
'You have much gold upon your head,'
They answered all together:
'Buy from us with a golden curl.'
She clipped a precious golden lock,
She dropped a tear more rare than pearl,
Then sucked their fruit globes fair or red:
Sweeter than honey from the rock.
Stronger than man-rejoicing wine,
Clearer than water flowed that juice;
She never tasted such before,
How should it cloy with length of use?
She sucked and sucked and sucked the more
Fruits which that unknown orchard bore;
She sucked until her lips were sore;
Then flung the emptied rinds away
But gathered up one kernel-stone,
And knew not was it night or day
As she turned home alone.
. . . .

'Nay, hush,' said Laura:
'Nay, hush, my sister:
I ate and ate my fill,
Yet my mouth waters still;
Tomorrow night I will
Buy more;' and kissed her.
'Have done with sorrow;
I'll bring you plums tomorrow
Fresh on their mother twigs,
Cherries worth getting;
You cannot think what figs
My teeth have met in,
What melons icy-cold
Piled on a dish of gold
Too huge for me to hold,
What peaches with a velvet nap,
Pellucid grapes without one seed:
Odorous indeed must be the mead
Whereon they grow, and pure the wave they drink
With lilies at the brink,
And sugar-sweet their sap.'

Golden head by golden head,
Like two pigeons in one nest
Folded in each other's wings,
They lay down in their curtained bed:
Like two blossoms on one stem,
Like two flakes of new-fall'n snow,
Like two wands of ivory
Tipped with gold for awful kings.
Moon and stars gazed in at them,
Wind sang to them lullaby,
Lumbering owls forbore to fly,
Not a bat flapped to and fro
Round their rest:
Cheek to cheek and breast to breast
Locked together in one nest.

Early in the morning
When the first cock crowed his warning,
Neat like bees, as sweet and busy,
Laura rose with Lizzie:
Fetched in honey, milked the cows,
Aired and set to rights the house,
Kneaded cakes of whitest wheat,
Cakes for dainty mouths to eat,
Next churned butter, whipped up cream,

Fed their poultry, sat and sewed;
Talked as modest maidens should:
Lizzie with an open heart,
Laura in an absent dream,
One content, one sick in part;
One warbling for the mere bright day's delight,
One longing for the night.

. . . .

FOR DISCUSSION: *Goblin Market*

a) The poem has an almost fairy-tale type of quality, the flavour of a children's tale: can you spot why?
b) Much of the poem's success can be attributed to its formal features: is there anything that strikes you about the form of the poem? Can you find any literary figures?
c) If the poem is read symbolically, what symbolic meaning would you attribute to the goblin men and their fruit?
d) Do you consider this poem to be typical of women's poetry? Why or why not?

PROJECT WORK: THE TOPICS OF WOMEN'S POETRY

In the course of this chapter, we have so far only looked at a couple of topics: Plath's and Sexton's descriptions of their experiences as psychiatric patients, and female friendship as seen by women poets as diverse as Æmilia Lanyer, Katherine Philips and Christina Rossetti. Read some more poems by women (you can check first in any poetry anthology that is at your disposal and then have a look at the anthologies we refer you to in the Further Reading section of this chapter) and see if you can identify other topics which women poets have been typically concerned with. Or do you notice any topics that do not seem specific to women writers, but whose treatment at the hands of women writers differs significantly from their treatment by male poets?

REWRITING MYTHOLOGY: SAME BUT DIFFERENT

To regard women's poetry only as *women's* poetry, putting the emphasis on the fact that it is written by *women* and forgetting that it is after all – and perhaps, first of all – *poetry*, can be very misleading or even dangerous. It may have the effect of confining women's poetry to a ghetto, to courses on poetry written by women taught by women teachers to women students and perhaps, in the minds of some, to a secondary stage of poetic production in the arena of literary history. It is important therefore to study women's poetry also as *poetry*, that is, as part of a poetic tradition (to see, for instance, whether it follows the conventions set up by previous poets or whether it challenges them; or to see whether it fits nicely into the panorama of contemporary poetry

or whether it sits uneasily within the poetic establishment of its time).
So it is important, in other words, to study poetry written by women
not only as 'women's poetry' but also as poetry which shares a poetic
heritage with poetry written by men.

Gender issues are inevitably tied in with issues of race and class:
differences between a poem written by a man and a poem written by
a woman are just as important as differences between poems written
by a white person and a black person, or differences between poems
written by someone born and raised in an upper- or middle-class
family and someone born and raised in a working-class family.

Anne Sexton's poetry, for instance, may at times have more in
common with the poetry of a Western white male such as William
Butler Yeats (1865–1939) than with poetry written by Afro-American
or working-class women. Following in the tradition of Virgil and
Ovid, Sexton sometimes uses poetry to tell a story. In the poem reproduced below, which is included in her collection *All My Pretty Ones*

Icarus
(1962), she re-tells the classical myth of Icarus, the son of Dedalus, a
Greek architect and inventor. Icarus attempted to fly like a bird with
wings made of feathers and wax which his father had put together. He
managed at first, but his desire to get close to the sun caused the wax
in his wings to melt, plunging him into the sea. This is how Sexton
rewrites the tale:

To a Friend Whose Work Has Come to Triumph

Consider Icarus, pasting those sticky wings on,
testing that strange little tug at his shoulder blade,
and think of that first flawless moment over the lawn
of the labyrinth. Think of the difference it made!
There below are the trees, as awkward as camels;
and here are the shocked starlings pumping past
and think of innocent Icarus who is doing quite well:
larger than a sail, over the fog and the blast
of the plushy ocean he goes. Admire his wings!
Feel the fire at his neck and see how casually
he glances up and is caught, wondrously tunneling
into that hot eye. Who cares that he fell back to the sea?
See him acclaiming the sun and come plunging down
while his sensible daddy goes straight into town.

Sexton's poem on Icarus' fall has a lot in common with a poem
by W.B. Yeats about another classical myth. In *The Tower* (1928),

Leda
Yeats included a poem about the story of Leda and Zeus: the poem
describes the moment in which Zeus, in the shape of a swan, covers
Leda. Yeats manages to recreate the occasion in all its beauty and
terror and at the same time he lucidly evokes the consequences of
such an act:

Leda and the Swan

A SUDDEN blow; the great wings beating still
Above the staggering girl, her thighs caressed
By the dark webs, her nape caught in his bill,
He holds her helpless breast upon his breast.

How can those terrified vague fingers push
The feathered glory from her loosening thighs?
And how can body, laid in that white rush,
But feel the strange heart beating where it lies?

A shudder in the loins engenders there
The broken wall, the burning roof and tower
And Agamemnon dead.
                              Being so caught up,
So mastered by the brute of the air,
Did she put on his knowledge with his power
Before the indifferent beak could let her drop?

Although not directly mentioned or alluded to in the poem, Helen
and her sister Clytemnestra are two of the four people 'engendered' in
this union. Clytemnestra will eventually become Agamemnon's wife
and his murderer. Helen, who marries Agamemnon's brother and
elopes with Paris, will be the spark that ignites the Trojan war. So the
Trojan war and Agamemnon's fate, which are superbly described in
just one line and a half ('The broken wall, the burning roof and tower/
And Agamemnon dead') (ll. 10–11) are telescopically seen as if they
had begun the moment Leda met the Swan.

Sexton's and Yeats' poems have a number of features in common.
Each focuses on the experience of the person who suffers the consequences of the action: Icarus and Leda. Sexton's poem describes the
first human flight from the point of view of Icarus, what he must have
thought and felt when he was flying and getting close to the sun. Yeats
similarly describes the rape from Leda's perspective: the fright, the
helplessness experienced by Leda. And both poems also foreground
at the end the detachment, the callous lack of concern of the active
participants, those who are ultimately responsible for the action:
Dedalus and Zeus.

REPRESENTING THE MYTH OF THE FALL: SOME VERSIONS OF EVE

We have just seen how the study of women's poetry should not be
confined to poems written by women because, just like men, women
poets are the inheritors of given cultural traditions, so that they may
write in relation to a poetic heritage which they share with male
poets. For the same reason, women's studies need not be reduced
to the study of women's writing: some women critics have been
very interested in the analysis of female figures in poetry written by
men. How are women portrayed in male-authored poems? What

characteristics are attributed to women through poetry? In *Paradise Lost* (1667), John Milton shows Eve, the first woman, at a moment when she is alone, thinking. She confides to us how she first discovered her own image in a brook:

That day I oft remember, when from sleep
I first awaked, and found myself reposed
Under a shade of flowers, much wondering where
And what I was, whence thither brought, and how.
Not distant far from thence a murmuring sound
Of waters issued from a cave and spread
Into a liquid plain, then stood unmoved
Pure as the expanse of heaven; I thither went
With unexperienced thought, and laid me down
On the green bank, to look into the clear
Smooth lake, that to me seemed another sky.
As I bent down to look, just opposite,
A shape within the watery gleam appeared
Bending to look on me, I started back,
It started back, but pleased I soon returned,
Pleased it returned as soon with answering looks
Of sympathy and love; there I had fixed
Mine eyes till now, and pined with vain desire,
Had not a voice thus warned me, What thou seest,
What there thou seest fair creature is thyself,
With thee it came and goes: but follow me,
And I will bring thee where no shadow stays
Thy coming, and thy soft embraces, he
Whose image thou art, him thou shalt enjoy
Inseparably thine, to him shalt bear
Multitudes like thyself, and thence be called
Mother of human race: what could I do,
But follow straight, invisibly thus led?

                                        (Book IV, ll. 449–76)

FOR DISCUSSION: Eve in *Paradise Lost*

a) Some women have seen in this passage a confirmation of Milton's misogyny: Eve is portrayed as stupid and vain. Do you agree? Where in the text is Eve shown to be silly and very pleased with her physical appearance?

b) To whom does the voice which 'warns' Eve belong? Is it the voice of Eve's conscience or the voice of God? The way in which you answer these questions affects the interpretation of the last two lines: is Eve directly responsible for her actions or is she being manipulated by God?

c) What do you think of the above passage as poetry? How effective is blank verse as a medium for narrative?

Later in the poem, Milton narrates the episode in which Eve eats the forbidden fruit: the earth shakes, and Milton portrays her as debating whether or not to let Adam partake of the knowledge she has obtained:

So saying, her rash hand in evil hour
Forth reaching to the fruit, she plucked, she ate:
Earth felt the wound, and nature from her seat
Sighing through all her works gave signs of woe,
That all was lost.
. . . .
    But to Adam in what sort
Shall I appear? Shall I to him make known
As yet my change, and give him to partake
Full happiness with me, or rather not,
But keep the odds of knowledge in my power
Without copartner? So to add what wants
In female sex, the more to draw his love,
And render me more equal, and perhaps,
A thing not undesirable, sometime
Superior; for inferior who is free?
          (Book IX, ll. 780–4; 816–25)

Milton's Eve appears here as a cunning seductress who plans to **Milton's Eve**
keep the knowledge she has obtained from the fruit in order 'the more
to draw his love'. Interestingly, so far in the poem, Eve has been
slightly stupid and as soon as she eats the fruit she becomes wily and
articulate. As can be seen when one compares this passage with the
one quoted above, her character has changed radically: the way she
speaks and her train of thought resemble those of Satan in earlier
books of the poem. Milton's Eve has become a rebellious figure, a
shrew, a virago. She is also portrayed as a threat to man and as man's
adversary, willing to compete with him and be his superior. In her
poem '*Salve Deus Rex Judaeorum*' (1611), Æmilia Lanyer gave a
slightly different version of Eve's character:

Our mother Eve, who tasted of the tree,
Giving to Adam what she held most dear,
Was simply good, and had no power to see;
The aftercoming harm did not appear.
The Subtile serpent that our sex betrayed
Before our fall so sure a plot had laid

That undiscerning ignorance perceived
No guile or craft that was by him intended;
For had she known of what we were bereaved,
To his request she had not condescended.
But she, poor soul, by cunning was deceived:

No hurt therein her harmless heart intended;
For she alleged God's word, which he denies,
That they should die, but even as gods be wise.

But surely Adam cannot be excused:
Her fault though great, yet he was most to blame;
What weakness offered, strength might have refused.
. . . .
And then to lay the fault on patience' back,
That we, poor women, must endure it all!
We know right well he did discretion lack,
Being not persuaded thereunto at all
If Eve did err, it was for knowledge' sake;
The fruit being fair persuaded him to fall:
No subtle serpent's falsehood did betray him;
If he would eat it, who had the power to stay him?

Not Eve, whose fault was only too much love,
Which made her give this present to her dear,
That what she tasted he likewise might prove,
Whereby his knowledge might become more clear:
He never sought her weakness to reprove
With those sharp words which he of God did hear.
Yet men will boast of knowledge, which he took
From Eve's fair hand, as from a learnèd book.

Lanyer's Eve   Lanyer's representation of Eve here is very different from Milton's. In Lanyer's poem, Eve is neither stupid nor vain, and if she ate the forbidden fruit it was because a trap was laid for her; she was deceived by the serpent. She is not scheming, artful or calculating as in Milton's poem, and she offers Adam the fruit out of love, because she wants to share the knowledge she has just obtained with her partner. Yet it is Eve who has traditionally been found guilty of not withstanding temptation, even though Adam, who was not tempted by any serpent-like Satan, was not able to resist eating it either. Eve is blamed for the sad fate of the human race, deprived of the Garden of Eden and forced to toil on Earth, yet men are proud of the knowledge they obtained thanks to her. Lanyer's analysis of the Christian myth of the Fall exposes the contradictions inherent in the received reading of the myth. She questions the traditional representation of Eve as the one to be blamed and thus challenges a literary tradition which starts with the Bible. Milton, who began to write *Paradise Lost* when Lanyer had already finished *Salve Deus Rex Judaeorum*, unimaginatively reuses the old stereotype of Eve as *femme fatale*.

PROJECT WORK: PORTRAITS OF WOMEN IN NARRATIVE POETRY

If you enjoyed the comparison between Lanyer's and Milton's Eve, you might design your own project work by first choosing several literary portraits of women in narrative poems from several periods and authors and then looking for similarities and differences. You could for example start with the portraits of the Wife of Bath and the Prioress in Chaucer's *The Canterbury Tales*; you could also explore the comic side in the portrayal of Venus in Shakespeare's *Venus and Adonis*, or study the representation of women in poems written by women, such as Elizabeth Barrett Browning's *Aurora Leigh*. Finally you could move on to the modernist period and post-1945 poetry and see what images of women, if any, you find in poems by T.S. Eliot, W.H. Auden, Philip Larkin, Derek Walcott or Seamus Heaney, and compare them with images of women in Emily Dickinson, Sylvia Plath, Anne Sexton, Elizabeth Jennings or Liz Lochhead.

PROJECT WORK: REWRITING MYTHOLOGY

Flip through any anthology of nineteenth- and twentieth-century poetry you have access to and see if you find poems which include a rewriting of a classical myth. Compare them with the poems in this chapter and with sixteenth-century versions of Ovidian *epyllia* (see Glossary), such as Shakespeare's *Venus and Adonis* and Marlowe's *Hero and Leander*. What are their similarities and differences with regard to purpose and tone? What is the point of re-telling an old, well-known story? What is the use the myth is put to in each poem? None of these questions has a simple, single answer, so we offer none here. If you can, discuss possible answers with fellow-students. If you do not have an opportunity to do this, remember that it is often useful to ask questions even if you do not reach a satisfactory answer, because in the process of asking yourself questions about a poem you may notice features of the poem which you were not initially aware of.

PROJECT WORK: INTERTEXTUALITY IN 'A KUMQUAT FOR JOHN KEATS'

In 'A Kumquat for John Keats' (1995), Tony Harrison not only pays homage to John Keats, but he also quotes from two of his poems, the 'Ode On Melancholy' and 'The Eve of St Agnes'. The links which exist between literary works, the debts poems have to other poems (whether openly acknowledged, as Harrison does in this poem, or not at all; whether conscious borrowings or unconscious echoes) are studied under the umbrella-term *intertextuality*. Harrison's poem quotes from Keats, and this quote helps us to understand the mood of Harrison's poem much better. His poem also has something in common with another poem by Keats, the ode 'To Autumn', which is studied in this book, and it recalls, whether intentionally or not, Rossetti's *Goblin Market*: the three poets exploit the pleasure to be found in the sensorial images that the names of fruits evoke, the pleasure of taste and texture. Try to find out as much as you can about Tony Harrison, Christina Rossetti and John Keats: find out at least when they lived, what their social, cultural and racial background was. Get hold of the full versions of these three poems and study them in order to establish in what ways they are similar and in what ways they are different. We are asking you, in fact, to study their intertextual relations on the one hand, and on the other, to see if these poems owe something to the gender, class and race of their authors, whether they owe something – for instance – to the fact that Keats is culturally conditioned by the historical time and literary period he lived in, Rossetti is gender-conditioned because she is a woman, and Harrison is socially conditioned because he writes from the perspective of a working-class background mixed with a university education.

ACTIVITY: EXERCISING CRITICAL JUDGEMENT

a) **Which of the poems quoted in this chapter do you prefer and why? Or, more generally: of all the poems quoted in this book, which do you prefer and why?**

b) **Did you use purely subjective criteria to justify your preferences when answering question (a)? Can you think of more objective criteria? Would the latter be based on the literary quality of the language of the poems and if so, what does this literary quality consist in? What else could they be based on: the universal significance of the poem's themes, the imaginativeness of its images, the elegance of its internal patterning, the unexpected or 'defamiliarizing' ways in which familiar things are presented or, perhaps more generally, the poem's wittiness – in the sense of both sharp intelligence and amusing originality?**

c) **Finally, compare your judgements with those of other readers (students, friends, teachers, critics, . . .). Is this a way of increasing the objectivity of critical judgements? Are there any consistent differences between the critical judgements of male and female readers?**

REFERENCES AND SUGGESTIONS FOR FURTHER READING

Anne Sexton's 'Old' and 'To a Friend Whose Work Has Come to Triumph' are included in *The Selected Poems of Anne Sexton*, ed. Diane Wood Middlebrook and Diana Hume George (Virago, 1991). 'Tulips' is part of Sylvia Plath's most famous book of verse *Ariel* (Faber, 1965: 36–7), a book which repays being read in its entirety. Most of the other poems by Æmilia Lanyer, Katherine Philips, Christina Rossetti, W.B. Yeats, John Milton and Tony Harrison that are quoted or referred to in this chapter can be found in Robert Clark and Thomas Healy, *The Arnold Anthology of British and Irish Literature in English* (Arnold, 1997). '*Salve Deus Rex Judaeorum*' by Æmilia Lanyer is reproduced in *The Penguin Book of Renaissance Verse 1509–1659*, ed. D. Norbrook and H.R. Woudhuysen (Penguin, 1992).

Two more specific poetry anthologies are Terence Dawson and Robert Scott Dupree, *Seventeenth-Century English Poetry* (Harvester Wheatsheaf,

1994) and Nalini Jain and John Richardson, *Eighteenth-Century English Poetry* (Harvester Wheatsheaf, 1994). Both are particularly student-friendly, as each poem has an introduction, bibliography and abundant notes.

Other anthologies that may be of interest to you when studying women's poetry include Germaine Greer, S. Hastings, J. Medoff and M. Sansone, *Kissing the Rod: An Anthology of Seventeenth-Century Women's Verse* (Virago, 1988), Roger Lonsdale, *Eighteenth-Century Women Poets* (Oxford University Press, 1990), Isobel Armstrong, Joseph Bristow and Cath Sharrock, *Nineteenth-Century Women Poets* (Clarendon Press, 1996) and Fleur Adcock, *The Faber Book of Twentieth-Century Women's Poetry* (Faber, 1987).

Finally, a seminal study on women's poetry is Sandra M. Gilbert and Susan Gubar, *Shakespeare's Sisters: Feminist Essays on Women Poets* (Indiana University Press, 1979). The introduction to this book is a very good place to start reading about why for a long time it has been said that there are no women poets of note and that women cannot or should not write poetry.

4

DEATH ON STAGE
Learning to Die in a Revenge Tragedy

English Renaissance tragedy was very much concerned with representations of death. How does one die? What does one say when one is about to expire? How does one learn to die? The plots of revenge tragedies offered plenty of opportunities for an exploration of the moment of death, since in most of them, the dramatic action is brought to a close with a heap of dead bodies on the stage-floor. Offering a spectacle of blood was one of the constitutive features of tragedy as a dramatic genre.

FOR DISCUSSION

Can you think of any other constitutive features of tragedy as a dramatic genre?

Senecan tragedy   In showing death taking place on stage, English tragedy departs from the classical tradition of the *Senecan tragedy*. In plays by Seneca, the gore takes place off-stage and it is communicated to the audience by means of a messenger who comes on stage to report it. Deaths and murders are thus not explicitly shown in front of the audience. English Renaissance tragedy followed this trend initially, as in *Gorboduc* (jointly written by two lawyer-gentlemen, Thomas Sackville and Thomas Norton), but it soon began to transfer the moment of death onto the stage. This tendency begins already in the Elizabethan period: Shakespeare's *Romeo and Juliet* and *Hamlet* end with the deaths of the main characters and their dead bodies preside over the plays' endings. The trend continues and increases in the Jacobean period, where one finds many tragedies, most of them revenge tragedies, which end with representations of the act of dying.

catharsis   Showing on stage the very moment of death had its functions. A Renaissance audience would easily have recognized the most important one: 'pictures' of death had a *cathartic* effect. The frightening spectacle of spilled blood would induce us to become better human beings. Together with this, it must also have had a less commendable function: to attract paying customers.

In English Renaissance tragedy, dying is inevitably connected with language. Renaissance tragic heroes and heroines die talking. This is how Hamlet dies:

HAMLET: I am dead, Horatio. Wretched Queen, adieu.
   You that look pale and tremble at this chance,
   That are but mutes or audience to this act,
   Had I but time – as this fell sergeant, Death,
   Is strict in his arrest – O, I could tell you –
   But let it be. Horatio, I am dead,
   Thou livest. Report me and my cause aright
   To the unsatisfied.
HORATIO: Never believe it.
   I am more an antique Roman than a Dane.
   Here's yet some liquor left.
HAMLET: As th'art a man
   Give me the cup. Let go, by Heaven I'll ha't.
   O God, Horatio, what a wounded name,
   Things standing thus unknown, shall I leave behind me.
   If thou didst ever hold me in thy heart,
   Absent thee from felicity awhile,
   And in this harsh world draw thy breath in pain
   To tell my story.   [A march afar off and shot within
                 What warlike noise is this?

                    Enter Osric
OSRIC: Young Fortinbras, with conquest come from Poland,
   To the ambassadors of England gives
   This warlike volley.
HAMLET: O, I die, Horatio.
   The potent poison quiet o'ercrows my spirit.
   I cannot live to hear the news from England,
   But I do prophesy th'election lights
   On Fortinbras. He has my dying voice.
   So tell him, with th'occurrents more and less
   Which have solicited – the rest is silence.
                                      [Dies
                              (V.ii.338–65)

a) **Think about what topics are uppermost in Hamlet's mind when he realizes he is about to die. What does he talk about? What does he ask Horatio to do?**
b) **Horatio tries to commit suicide and Hamlet dissuades him from going ahead. How does he do it? What is the most important reason why Hamlet thinks Horatio should not kill himself?**
c) **Religion seems to be absent from Hamlet's thoughts: he does not pray, he does not let us know if he believes in hell, heaven or life after death. He only says, 'the rest is silence.' How do you interpret this?**

DISCUSSION

For someone who is under the effects of poison, who has just learned that he is going to die, Hamlet has his self-control and his mental faculties admirably about him. He also does a great deal of talking. We know that he is dying because while he talks, he keeps reminding us of it: 'I am dead, Horatio', 'Horatio, I am dead', 'O, I die, Horatio'. At times, realism was the least important of the preoccupations of Renaissance authors and audiences. This is however an important point in the play: death is a serious moment. Shakespeare wants his audience to listen with all five senses, so he strategically places a line addressed both to those witnessing Hamlet's death in the fictive world of the stage and in the real world of the pit and the galleries: 'You that look pale and tremble at this chance,/ That are but mutes or audience to this act'.

Hamlet's death is the death of a Renaissance man. Hamlet's story belongs to the legendary past of the Scandinavian countries, but Hamlet dies worrying about things which are very much the concern of a man who lives in England at the beginning of the seventeenth century: he dies almost as a Renaissance prince. The only thing that is missing from Hamlet's death to make it an exemplary Renaissance death is religion. What does Hamlet talk about in this climactic moment? Mostly, about three things: his reputation, politics and his love for Horatio.

The approach of death makes Hamlet consider, first of all, his reputation: if the story of his father's murder is not known, he will be thought of as his uncle's murderer and, even worse, as a regicide. In the Renaissance, when the divine right of monarchs was still very much an issue, killing a king was not only a political act, but also an act which defied God's authority. This is why Hamlet entreats Horatio: 'Report me and my cause aright/ To the unsatisfied'. The Renaissance man was much concerned with 'fame', with the fate of his public image after his death. Immortality was often understood as the good reputation one leaves behind. This is why Hamlet pleads with Horatio and asks him not to commit suicide so that he can tell his story: 'Give me the cup. Let go, by Heaven I'll ha't./ O God, Horatio, what a wounded name,/ Things standing thus unknown, shall I leave behind me.' Hamlet snatches the cup containing the remaining poison from Horatio's hand. He drinks it, so that Horatio cannot kill himself. Horatio has to live to clear Hamlet's name.

Politics is the second thing that worries Hamlet when he is about to die. In fact, in the very last seconds of his life, Hamlet is also very concerned with the fate of his country. When he is told that Fortinbras is coming, he remembers Denmark is an elected monarchy, and he tells Horatio that his vote goes to Fortinbras: 'He has my dying voice'. So in effect, the last thing Hamlet does before he dies is to perform a civic act: he casts his ballot.

The third thing he does before dying is to spare a few seconds for the lyrical: 'If thou didst ever hold me in thy heart,/ Absent thee from felicity awhile,/ And in this harsh world draw thy breath in pain/ To tell my story.' Hamlet manipulates Horatio's feelings and asks him, if he ever loved him, to face pain and suffering for the sake of clearing Hamlet's reputation. The representation of Hamlet's death exploits pathos and emotion through language, and then Hamlet dies and death brings silence.

John Webster (1580?–1634?) may have learnt the art of representing death from Shakespeare's works, from plays he saw staged or from public executions. Until recently, very little was known about him: now it is known that his father was renowned in London for his business in wagons, carts and coaches, and probably this had put him in contact since youth with both players and death. There are records showing that his father had dealings with theatrical companies, and condemned men from Newgate prison used the Websters' service in their last journey. Webster collaborated with other playwrights in several plays, but there are two which are attributed entirely to him, *The White Devil* (1608) and *The Duchess of Malfi* (c.1614). In these two plays, Webster developed a knack for creating memorable characters out of the words they speak. When driven to the verge of madness by her enemies, the Duchess of Malfi simply says: 'I am the Duchess of Malfi still'. With this sentence Webster offers her character in its quintessence: a proud, strong woman, used to being obeyed, who refuses to face the obviousness of her impending death while she still is, officially, the head of state. Once known, Webster's characters remain in our memory as remarkable speakers.

EXPLOITING PATHOS THROUGH LANGUAGE

Webster has been accused, however, of having at times little control over dramatic structure: his plays are 'episodic', full of memorable scenes, of breath-taking moments. If this is a defect, it can also be shown to be an advantage: what his plays lose in 'tightness' they gain, at times, in 'intensity'. In *The White Devil*, when Isabella dies, her son Giovanni says to Francisco, the duke of Florence:

GIOVANNI: What do the dead do, uncle? do they eat,
   Hear music, go a-hunting, and be merry,
   As we that live?
FRANCESCO: No coz; they sleep.
GIOVANNI: Lord, Lord, that I were dead –
   I have not slept these six nights. When do they wake?
FRANCESCO: When God shall please.
GIOVANNI: Good God let her sleep ever.
   For I have known her wake an hundred nights,
   When all the pillow, where she laid her head,
   Was brine-wet with her tears.

I am to complain to you sir.
I'll tell you how they have used her now she's dead:
They wrapp'd her in a cruel fold of lead
And would not let me kiss her.
                                            (III.ii.321–32)

In what ways is Giovanni's attitude to death different from Hamlet's?

DISCUSSION	Giovanni's preoccupation with life after death ('What do the dead do?') signals a departure from Hamlet's attitude to death: Giovanni introduces metaphysical worries which did not exist in Hamlet's mind at that moment. For Hamlet, as for another Renaissance man, Montaigne, death is somehow like sleep: 'To die, to sleep;/ To sleep, perchance to dream . . . / For in that sleep of death what dreams may come' (III.i.64–6). Giovanni's uncle, Francesco, shares this view of death with Hamlet and Montaigne. Giovanni is a child whose naïvety prompts him to ask: 'do they eat,/ Hear music, go a-hunting, and be merry,/ As we that live?' Giovanni's reflection about the dead has now become a thought about the living: Webster puts in the child's mouth a description of the living which does not apply to Giovanni and Francesco themselves, who are mourning the death of Isabella. This split between what the living should do (eat, hear music, go hunting, be merry) and what they actually do (mourn a close relative, be unable to sleep at night, shed tears on one's pillow, put a mother in a lead coffin, prevent a child from kissing his mother) aims to arise feelings of sadness and pity in the audience – or, to put it in technical terms, it aims to
pathos	create *pathos*.

**DEATH
AND ITS
METAPHORS**

Webster, as we have just seen, can arrest the action of his plays easily and exploit the pathos or the terror of the experience of death for poetic effect. This is often the case when Webster decides to represent the death of one – or several – characters, something which is part and parcel of the plot of a revenge tragedy. In Webster, the moment of death – the dying speech of a character on stage – is a time for poetry.

When Webster's characters are about to die, their speech often fills with poetic images, metaphors, comparisons and imaginative descriptions of what they are experiencing. At the same time, the representation of the moment of death usually rests on a handful of images: death as a journey, death as darkness and death as silence. In *The White Devil*, just before being killed by Lodovico and the conspirators, Vittoria and Zanche are asked by Vittoria's brother Flamineo to commit suicide by shooting each other. Flamineo arranges for Vittoria and her maid to shoot him, after making them swear that they will then shoot each other and keep him company in death. They shoot him but then refuse to shoot each other and Flamineo complains of their perjury and unfaithfulness. In the end, it will transpire that Flamineo is not wounded at all because the pistols were not charged, but this is only known after he has 'represented' his own death. In the course of Flamineo's feigned death, dying is presented as a *journey*, either to hell or heaven. When Flamineo insists on persuading her to fulfil her promise of joining him in death, Vittoria says to him: 'Think whither thou art going' (V.vi.128), and a little later they have the following exchange:

death as a journey

FLAMINEO: O the way's dark and horrid! I cannot see,
    Shall I have no company?
VITTORIA: O yes thy sins
    Do run before thee to fetch fire from hell,
    To light thee thither.

                              (V.vi.136–9)

Both Vittoria and Flamineo equate death with a journey and dying with travelling. Vittoria, still ignoring that her brother's death is feigned, makes the most of the opportunity to show that she does not entertain any doubts regarding the destination her brother is travelling to. When both of them are killed a little later, this time for real, they settle for the same metaphor and speak of death as a journey with an unknown terminus. Vittoria, for example, says: 'My soul, like to a ship in a black storm,/ Is driven, I know not whither' (V.vi.246–7).

The scene of Flamineo's feigned death also makes use of the sudden oncoming of *darkness* as a powerful image of what dying is like: the way is 'dark and horrid', says Flamineo, and then adds, 'I cannot see'. Flamineo's real death presents the act of dying as the arrival of *silence*: death is the end of conversation. When he is about to die, he refuses to talk or to think and begins to feel dumbness overpowering him. Flamineo dies, like Hamlet, reminding us that death means silence:

death as darkness

death as silence

I am i'th'way to study a long silence,
To prate were idle, – I remember nothing.
There's nothing of so infinite vexation
As man's own thoughts.

                              (V.vi.201–4)

My life was a black charnel. I have caught
An everlasting cold; I have lost my voice
Most irrecoverably. Farewell, glorious villain
                              (V.vi.268–70)

In *The Duchess of Malfi*, the death of the Machiavellian character in the play, Bosola, is another occasion to explore the accoutrements of death. Bosola has killed Antonio by mistake (he thought he was killing

Ferdinand), and when asked just before he dies 'How came Antonio by his death?' he replies:

> BOSOLA: In a mist: I know not how –
>   Such a mistake as I have often seen
>   In a play: – O, I am gone! –
>   We are only like dead walls, or vaulted graves,
>   That ruin'd, yield no echo: – Fare you well –
>   It may be pain, but no harm to me to die
>   In so good a quarrel. O, this gloomy world!
>   In what a shadow, or deep pit of darkness,
>   Doth womanish and fearful mankind live!
>   Let worthy minds ne'er stagger in distrust
>   To suffer death, or shame for what is just –
>   Mine is another voyage.
>
> (V.v.94–105)

a) Compare what Bosola and Flamineo talk about when they are about to die. Is death portrayed in the same way in their speeches? (Look out for metaphors involving concepts such as travelling, darkness and silence.)

b) Do Bosola's and Flamineo's dying speeches resemble Hamlet's? Do they worry about the same things when they are about to die?

DISCUSSION

a) Renaissance audiences could shift from laughter to tears in a split second: the first two and a half lines of Bosola's speech should perhaps make you smile, because they are a threat to the suspension of disbelief by reminding us we are just watching a play, but the rest of the speech should turn your mind to things sad, melancholic and metaphysical. In the dying speeches of both Bosola and Flamineo death is portrayed as bringing the loss of three human faculties (seeing, speaking, knowing), and the representation of death on stage assumes the shape of a silent, dark journey into an unknown wilderness. When they have the first intimations that they are going to die, both Bosola and Flamineo use the metaphor of death as a journey, a journey which affords no companion but darkness and silence: in his feigned death, Flamineo says 'O the way's dark and horrid! I cannot see,' while Bosola exclaims 'O, I am gone', meaning 'I die', and describes death as a 'voyage'. Both of them also equate death with silence: for Flamineo, to die is to lose one's voice; for Bosola, to be dead means not to be able to produce sound, to 'yield no echo'.

b) The deaths of Bosola and Flamineo recall Hamlet's death in some ways. In his moving speech to his friend Horatio, Hamlet refers to life on earth as this 'harsh world'. Flamineo describes his life as 'a black charnel' and Bosola sounds as if he is glossing Hamlet when he says 'O, this gloomy world!/ In what a shadow, or deep pit of darkness,/ Doth womanish and fearful mankind live!' Hamlet's description of death as silence ('The rest is silence') is appropriated by both Bosola and Flamineo: Bosola compares the dead with ruined vaults which have no echo ('We are only like dead walls, or vaulted graves,/ That ruin'd, yield no echo'), and Flamineo describes life after death as the study of silence ('I am i'th'way to study a long silence,/ To prate were idle'). For Flamineo, dying is to lose one's voice 'irrecoverably'. However, the representation of the deaths of Bosola and Flamineo is very different from Hamlet's act of dying in other respects. Hamlet dies thinking mostly about his reputation and the fate of the throne of Denmark: he is concerned with what he leaves behind, but he does not worry about what happens to the dead after death, he does not spare a thought for the issue of where the soul goes when the body dies. He conceives of death as rest, as the end of troubles and anxiety, as the arrival of happiness; and this is why he says to Horatio, 'Absent thee from felicity awhile'. Bosola and Flamineo, on the other hand, are very worried about the fate of their soul after death: they see death as a journey through obscurity, a journey with an unknown destination. Unlike Hamlet, Bosola and Flamineo regard death as an unpleasant experience, full of horror and anxiety.

WOMEN WELCOMING DEATH IN *THE WHITE DEVIL*

The White Devil deals with events that took place in Italy in 1581–5: the story of the illicit love the Duke of Brachiano feels for Vittoria Corombona, the wife of Camillo. Vittoria's brother, Flamineo, engineers the death of Camillo and helps Brachiano to seduce Vittoria. After a quarrel, Flamineo kills his brother Marcello, who is virtuous and disapproves of Flamineo's Machiavellism. Brachiano has killed his own wife Isabella, the sister of the Duke of Florence, in order to carry out his 'unlawful purpose' and marry Vittoria. Revenge inevitably ensues: Brachiano will be poisoned by Isabella's brother and Vittoria and Flamineo will be murdered.

Although the plot is perhaps neither better nor worse than many revenge plays, Webster's ability to trace psychologically interesting characters with his poetic, often lyrical style raises this play far above other Jacobean tragedies. Vittoria Corombona is one of these characters, finely sketched, retaining her dignity and pride in the very face of death. When her executioner approaches she accosts him with these words:

VITTORIA: You, my death's man:
   Methinks thou dost not look horrid enough,
   Thou hast too good a face to be a hangman, –
   If thou be, do thy office in right form;
   Fall down upon thy knees and ask forgiveness.
LODOVICO: O thou hast been a most prodigious comet,
   But I'll cut off your train: – kill the Moor first.

> VITTORIA: You shall not kill her first. Behold my breast, –
>   I will be waited on in death; my servant
>   Shall never go before me.
> GASPARO: Are you so brave?
> VITTORIA: Yes I shall welcome death
>   As princes do some great ambassadors;
>   I'll meet thy weapon half way.
>   (V.vi.207–19)

a) **Vittoria's brave attitude towards her murderers is manifested through her sense of humour even if, given the circumstances, it is a sort of 'black' humour. See if you can detect the comic side of this passage and explain its function at this tragic climax of the play.**

b) **At a moment such as this, one might not expect those who are about to die to be worried about social status and hierarchy, about deference and ceremonial matters. Yet Vittoria seems to be. Underline the passage where she demands to be treated according to her rank. Why are power relations important to her at the moment of death?**

DISCUSSION

a) Vittoria's humour, which fills most of the first of her three speeches at this crucial point in her life, shows her murderers that she is not frightened. She makes fun of one of them by questioning his fitness for the job; he is not professional enough ('Thou hast too good a face to be a hangman'), he does not look frightening ('Methinks thou dost not look horrid enough'), he does not follow the steps in the executioner's handbook ('do thy office in right form'). The executioner has to ask forgiveness because he is simply the medium through which the sentence is carried out: by putting Lodovico in the position of someone hired to kill she is insulting him. She treats him as she would treat someone working for her: 'You, my death's man'. In fact, the word 'man' in Elizabethan English can mean 'servant', so my 'death's man' can be read both as my 'manservant' for death-related matters and as death's servant. On top of this, she gives him an order to kneel down in front of her in order to emphasize his subordinate status, to point out that although she is about to die she is still his superior. She shows that she is still in possession of the imperative-laden language of the powerful: 'Fall down upon thy knees and ask forgiveness'. So Vittoria's choice of language, at this time of death, serves to exhibit valour and display power and rank.

black humour

power relations

b) Vittoria's interest in having her social status acknowledged might be thought to be ridiculous: what is the point, if she is about to die? Rather than seeming useless, however, her pride and preoccupation with rank raise the pathos of her death-scene. She scores for being brave, so the audience feels she does not deserve her end. Yet her pride simultaneously offers an insight into the human condition: how difficult it is, even in the sight of imminent death, to let human worries go, how hard it is to accept that one is going to die and nothing matters any more.

The Duchess of Malfi is also a revenge play, but with a less convoluted plot than *The White Devil*. The Duchess, a young widow, has two brothers, Ferdinand and the Cardinal, both of whom forbid her to marry again (the motive is not clear: at some point, matters of honour seem to be in play; but greed to control and possess her wealth after her death are also mentioned). She ignores their threats and secretly marries her steward and secretary, Antonio, after proposing to him in a memorable scene. Her brothers, who disapprove strongly of this mésalliance, prepare all sorts of psychological torture for her: they show her wax figures which make her believe her sons and husband are dead, they surround her with deranged people brought from a mad-house. In the midst of all the terror-inspiring horrors they entertain her with in her imprisonment, the Duchess retains her dignity. Her brothers will eventually have her killed; they send Bosola, their Machiavellian right hand, to strangle her and two of her children. Revenge and murder will follow. One of the murdering brothers, Ferdinand, repents having instigated his sister's death as soon as he beholds her dead and becomes mentally disturbed. He produces one of the most breathtaking lines in the play: 'Cover her face; mine eyes dazzle: she died young' (IV.ii.263). He refuses to pay Bosola for his services, accuses him of killing the Duchess and kindles in him the desire for revenge. In the end Bosola will kill the Cardinal, and Ferdinand and Bosola will kill each other.

THE MANNER OF DYING IN *THE DUCHESS OF MALFI*

As a revenge play, it is an interesting *tour de force*, because the man who actually kills the Duchess, although acting as a deputy murderer for her brothers, will be the same man who takes upon himself the duty of carrying out her revenge. As soon as she is dead, one of the brothers repents and blames the murderer for carrying out his orders: he will revenge his sister's death on her material executioner. So both the instigator and the actual murderer will kill each other and become revengers as well as murderers.

A good share of the interest the play has for the study of the representation of death lies, as in *The White Devil*, in individual episodes which bring the action momentarily to a halt so that poetry and pathos can be displayed. The scene of the Duchess's death is a good example; her executioners will be able to kill her, but they will not succeed in their attempt to terrify her:

BOSOLA: Doth not death fright you?
DUCHESS: Who would be afraid on't?
   Knowing to meet such excellent company
   In the other world.
BOSOLA: Yet, methinks,

> The manner of your death should much afflict you,
> This cord should terrify you?
> DUCHESS: Not a whit:
> What would it pleasure me to have my throat cut
> With diamonds? or to be smothered
> With cassia? or to be shot to death with pearls?
> I know death hath ten thousand several doors
> For men to take their exits
>
>   (IV.ii.211–20)

The Duchess, in fact, dies ruling the state. She is the head of state so she is the one responsible for decreeing death-warrants. She is the one who gives the order for her own capital punishment. She is so used to giving orders that even her last speech on stage is full of commands, of imperatives:

> DUCHESS: Pull, and pull strongly, for your able strength
> Must pull down heaven upon me:
> Yet stay; heaven-gates are not so highly arch'd
> As princes' palaces, they that enter there
> Must go upon their knees – Come violent death,
> Serve for mandragora to make me sleep!
> Go tell my brothers, when I am laid out,
> They then may feed in quiet.
>
>   (IV.ii.230–7)

Compare the death of the Duchess of Malfi with the death of Vittoria in _The White Devil_. Do you notice any similarities? And any differences?

DISCUSSION

language of the powerful

Like Vittoria, the Duchess addresses her murderer with the _language of the powerful_: both of them make generous use of imperatives. The Duchess gives Bosola the order to go ahead, 'Pull, and pull strongly,' and then tells him to wait, 'Yet stay'. She even gives a command to Death itself, 'Come violent death,' and then a new command for Bosola, 'Go tell my brothers'. Neither Vittoria nor the Duchess let their executioners frighten them: the killers cannot inspire terror in their victims. Both Vittoria and the Duchess only have scorn and contempt for those who try to terrify them. There is a difference, however, in the way Vittoria and the Duchess welcome death. While Vittoria meets her death proud as ever and comparing herself to a prince who meets an ambassador, the Duchess teaches us humility by means of kneeling. Vittoria takes pains to assert her rank, whereas the Duchess, who is to the very moment of her death the head of state, need not strive to establish her status. Instead, she kneels and dies, like a true Renaissance prince, in the act of praying.

PROJECT WORK: PICTURES OF DEATH

a) Webster was not the only Jacobean playwright to show strong, articulate women dying on stage. Compare the deaths of Vittoria and the Duchess of Malfi with the deaths of Bianca and Beatrice in Middleton's *Women Beware Women* (Act V, Scene ii, ll. 184–221) and *The Changeling* (Act V, Scene iii, ll. 149–79).

b) Hamlet, the prince of Denmark, dies before getting a chance to be elected king of his country but in some ways he dies as a monarch. His death is given much more room in the play than the death of the ruling monarch, his uncle Claudio. Hamlet's death has much in common with the deaths of tragic monarchs – and yet it is different in some respects. Try to establish the similarities and differences which obtain between the death of Hamlet and the deaths of other famous tragic figures of the Early Modern English stage, such as Marlowe's Tamburlaine, Marlowe's Edward II, Shakespeare's Richard II or Shakespeare's Richard III.

c) If you want to make a more comprehensive study of the different ways in which Renaissance playwrights approached the representation of death on stage, you could put together a portfolio of death scenes from Elizabethan and Jacobean tragedies. Shakespeare's *Richard II* and Marlowe's *Edward II*, two plays which deal with kings who were deposed and later killed, offer a good starting-point. The death of the eponymous hero in Marlowe's *Dr. Faustus*, and the horror he feels when the spirits come to take him to hell, can be compared to the serenity of the Duchess at the moment of death. Other plays you may scan in search of death scenes are domestic revenge tragedies, such as Thomas Middleton's *Women Beware Women* and *The Changeling*, John Ford's *'Tis Pity She's a Whore*, Thomas Heywood's *A Woman Killed with Kindness*, and the anonymous *The Revenger's Tragedy* (often attributed to either Middleton or Cyril Tourneur). Once you have compiled your portfolio, you could search your death scenes for similarities and differences amongst them, so that you can establish what 'pictures of death' could be seen on the Early Modern English stage. Another path you may want to pursue in your study is the connection between death and language: what do characters say when they are about to die? How does what a dying character says either confirm or subvert what a playgoer sees depicted on the stage?

PROJECT WORK: INCEST AND MARRIAGE IN DOMESTIC TRAGEDY

Many Jacobean tragedies are described as 'domestic' tragedies because they often depict the lives and deaths of men and women who are neither classical heroes nor kings and queens. These domestic tragedies show how sometimes the rupture of domestic peace can lead to a tragic dénouement in the family and the home. You could make use of the domestic tragedies listed above for an in-depth study of two topics which recur in Jacobean tragedies: incest and marriage. The Jacobean interest in incestuous relationships can be explored in Webster's *The Duchess of*

Malfi and Ford's *'Tis Pity She's a Whore*; you could, for instance, attempt to determine to what extent these plays project different attitudes towards incest. Alternatively, you could study representations of married life in Jacobean domestic tragedies. Jacobean playwrights seem to have been very interested in the fragility of marriage, so many plays of the period discuss issues such as marital faithfulness, jealousy, honour, and the social constraints in which married couples are entangled. Middleton's *Women Beware Women* and *The Changeling* can be studied alongside Heywood's *A Woman Killed with Kindness*, Webster's *The White Devil* and Shakespeare's *The Winter's Tale* to show how in Jacobean tragedy marital happiness, whether it is linked to individual will or social codes of conduct, is always brittle.

PROJECT WORK: IMAGES OF LOVE AND LIFE

How is love represented in Shakespeare's *Romeo and Juliet* and/or *Antony and Cleopatra*? Study what images Shakespeare uses to describe love in these plays. Alternatively, you could study what images are used to describe life in *Macbeth*. A good starting-point for the latter project would be the extract from *Macbeth* quoted on p. 105, but you should also have a look at the other soliloquies spoken by Macbeth in the play. Finally, prepare a brief essay on your chosen topic, taking the section on 'Death and its metaphors', p. 58 as a guide. Also read chapter 8 of this book, where you will find further information about metaphor analysis.

REFERENCES AND SUGGESTIONS FOR FURTHER READING

Quotations from *The White Devil* and *The Duchess of Malfi* have been taken from D.C. Gunby's editions of the plays in John Webster, *Three Plays* (Penguin, 1972). Both plays have also been edited by J.R. Brown for The Revels Plays and by E. Brennan for the New Mermaids series. Don D. Moore, *Webster: The Critical Heritage* (Routledge and Kegan Paul, 1981) is a very good source of information about the critical history of the plays. Muriel Bradbrook's *John Webster: Citizen and Dramatist* (Weidenfeld and Nicolson, 1980) contains much valuable information about the playwright. Two good articles on each of the plays studied in this chapter are Lisa Jardine, '"I Am the Duchess of Malfi Still": Wealth, Inheritance and the Spectre of Strong Women. Coda: Hic Mulier: Female Bogey', in *Still Harping on Daughters: Women and Drama in the Age of Shakespeare* (Harvester, 1983: 68–102) and Ann Rosalind Jones, 'Italian and Others: *The White Devil*', in David Scott Kastan and Peter Stallybrass (eds) *Staging the Renaissance: Reinterpretations of Elizabethan and Jacobean Drama* (Routledge, 1991: 251–62). As for *Hamlet*, an indispensable introduction is Ann Thompson and Neil Taylor, *William Shakespeare: Hamlet* in the Writers and their Work series (Northcote House and the British Council, 1996).

For those wanting to read about tragedy in general a good place to start is Robert Watson's 'Tragedy', in A.R. Braunmuller and Michael Hattaway (eds) *The Cambridge Companion to English Renaissance Drama* (Cambridge

University Press, 1990). Some important contributions to Renaissance tragedy are Catherine Belsey, *The Subject of Tragedy: Identity and Difference in Renaissance Drama* (Routledge, 1985), Dympna Callaghan, *Woman and Gender in Renaissance Tragedy* (Harvester Wheatsheaf, 1989) and Jonathan Dollimore, *Radical Tragedy: Religion, Ideology and Power in the Drama of Shakespeare and his Contemporaries* (Harvester Wheatsheaf, 1989).

5

SHERIDAN'S SCHOOL FOR MARRIAGE

The Effect of Education and the Nature of Comedy

tragedy vs. comedy

In his poem *Don Juan*, the Romantic poet Lord Byron succinctly puts the difference between *tragedy* and *comedy*:

All tragedies are finished by a death
All comedies are ended by a marriage

Byron's lines encapsulate one of the differences between tragedies and comedies which critics have repeatedly noted: comedies have a happy ending, whereas tragedies do not. Byron's definitions rest on a long-established practice of regarding tragedy and comedy as two well-differentiated, almost incompatible dramatic genres: since classical Greek drama, many have thought that whereas tragedy moves us and fills us with fear or pity, comedy simply leads to laughter. Comedy is often defined by its relation to tragedy and it is usually seen as its opposite. The French philosopher Henri Bergson, for example, has defined comedy as an inversion of tragedy: according to this vision of comedy, Shylock in Shakespeare's *The Merchant of Venice* is comic because he is a villain whose villainy has turned upon himself. The eighteenth-century English writer Horace Walpole thought that tragedy makes us feel and comedy makes us think.

Distinctions between tragedy and comedy are also entangled with questions of status and value. For Ben Jonson, the Renaissance poet and playwright, the difference between tragedy and comedy is one of subject-matter: tragedy addresses the issue of crime and serious offences but comedy only deals with human folly. Is tragedy then superior to comedy? Throughout the centuries, many have thought so because, they argue, tragedy appeals to our nobler ideas and feelings. Tragedy aims to make better human beings of us. Comedy, instead, only takes us nearer to the contemptible, to what we ought to despise. Comedy only aims to amuse us. Needless to say, not everybody agrees.

This strict separation between laughter as the target of comedy and feeling as the purpose of tragedy stems from the theoretical reflections of the Greek philosopher Aristotle and has sometimes been used uncritically. In fact, the history of world theatre shows that tragedy and comedy do not always exist separately from one another. *The Merchant of Venice* does not have a truly happy ending if Shylock's tragic fate is read as unfair, and the so-called 'porter scene' in *Macbeth* reminds us that comedy and laughter are sometimes present in the midst of tragedy. Yet in spite of this possible grafting of unhappiness onto comedy and laughter onto tragedy, Byron's words carry a lot of sense: most tragedies, if not all, are very much concerned with death, as we have just seen in the previous chapter, and many comedies, as Shakespearean comedy shows, have much to do with marriage. If a tragedy often shows its audience how to learn to die, a comedy can be turned into a school for marriage.

One of Richard Brinsley Sheridan's comedies, *The Rivals* (1775), is in fact mostly about marriage. It discusses the principles which one ought and ought not to follow when choosing a partner. Should one marry for love or for money? Should one marry whom one pleases or listen to the opinion of one's next of kin? Sheridan's comedy seems to take to task both those who oppose the individual's free choice and those who marry purely for passion and sentiment. Sheridan also discusses how one can get some guidance to make the right choice. He wrote his comedies at a time when a new literary genre had just emerged and threatened to displace the theatre: his plays are contemporaneous with the rise of the novel. One of the questions to be answered in Sheridan's school for marriage is: do novels help us with our sentimental education?

The Rivals gets its name from the suitors who compete for the hand of the play's heroine, Lydia Languish. Most of the play's intrigue rests on the double identity of one of Lydia's suitors: Captain Absolute, who is courting Lydia under a disguised identity, Ensign Beverley. Lydia has read too many novels: she wants to marry for love, and is afraid that those who court her do so for her 'portion' (the money she will inherit when she comes of age). Being aware of this, Absolute, who is also heir to a fortune, decides to court her under the pretended identity of a poor soldier, who is prepared to elope with her and marry her without her fortune. Lydia is at present the ward of a widowed aunt, Mrs Malaprop, who tries to do her best to prevent Lydia from reading novels and receiving visits from Beverley.

Mrs Malaprop gets all sorts of difficult words wrong and has given the English language the word *malapropism*. She is, in fact, as central **malapropism** a character in the play as either of the two lovers, Lydia and Absolute. Act I, Scene ii begins with Lucy, Lydia's maid, returning from the circulating library where she has gone to fetch novels for her lady; suddenly, Mrs Malaprop and Sir Anthony Absolute, Captain Absolute's father, turn up and begin to climb the staircase to Lydia's bedroom. Lydia's cousin, Julia, has to be hurried away by means of another route, the hidden staircase used by serving-maids, so that Mrs Malaprop and Sir Anthony do not bump into her. Most importantly, books of a certain kind have to be hidden and books of a very different nature displayed.

Read the passage below and think about the following questions:

a) **What is the difference between the books Lydia tells Lucy to hide and those she tells her to display? What does the fact that the hairdresser has used Fordyce's *Sermons* up to 'Proper Pride' tell us?**

b) **What is Lydia like? What do we learn about her from her own words?**

c) **What are Lydia's views of marriage?**

LUCY: O Lud! Ma'am, they are both coming upstairs.

LYDIA: Well, I'll not detain you coz – adieu, my dear Julia, I'm sure you are in haste to send to Faulkland. There – through my room you'll find another staircase.

JULIA: Adieu. [*Embrace*]   [*Exit Julia*

LYDIA: Here, my dear Lucy, hide these books – quick, quick – fling *Peregrine Pickle* under the toilet – throw *Roderick Random* into the closet – put *The Innocent Adultery* into *The Whole Duty of Man* – thrust *Lord Aimworth* under the sofa – cram Ovid behind the bolster – there – put *The Man of Feeling* into your pocket – so, so, now lay Mrs Chapone in sight, and leave Fordyce's *Sermons* open on the table.

LUCY: O burn it, Ma'am, the hairdresser has torn away as far as 'Proper Pride'.

LYDIA: Never mind – open at 'Sobriety' – fling me Lord Chesterfield's *Letters*. Now for 'em.

Enter Mrs Malaprop and Sir Anthony Absolute

MRS MALAPROP: There, Sir Anthony, there sits the deliberate simpleton, who wants to disgrace her family, and lavish herself on a fellow not worth a shilling!

LYDIA: Madam, I thought you once –

MRS MALAPROP: You thought, Miss! I don't know any business you have to think at all – thought does not become a young woman; the point we would request of you is, that you promise to forget this fellow – to illiterate him, I say, quite from your memory.

LYDIA: Ah! Madam! Our memories are independent of our wills. It is not so easy to forget.

MRS MALAPROP: But I say it is, Miss; there is nothing on earth so easy as to forget, if a person chooses to set about it. I'm sure I have as much forgot your poor uncle as if he had never existed – and I thought it my duty so to do; and let me tell you, Lydia, these violent memories don't become a young woman.

SIR ANTHONY: Why sure she won't pretend to remember what she's ordered not! Aye, this comes of her reading!

LYDIA: What crime, Madam, have I committed to be treated thus?

MRS MALAPROP: Now don't attempt to extirpate yourself from the matter; you know I have proof controvertible of it. But tell me, will you promise to do as you're bid? Will you take a husband of your friend's choosing?

LYDIA: Madam, I must tell you plainly, that had I no preference for anyone else, the choice you have made would be my aversion.

MRS MALAPROP: What business have you, Miss, with *preference* and *aversion*? They don't become a young woman; and you ought to know, that as both always wear off, 'tis safest in matrimony to begin with a little aversion. I am sure I hated your poor dear uncle before marriage as if he'd been a blackamoor – and yet, Miss, you are sensible what a wife I made! – and when it pleased Heaven to release me from him, 'tis unknown what tears I shed! But suppose we were going to give you another choice, will you promise us to give up this Beverley?

LYDIA: Could I belie my thoughts so far, as to give that promise, my actions would certainly as far belie my words.

MRS MALAPROP: Take yourself to your room. You are fit company for nothing but your own ill-humours.

LYDIA: Willingly, Ma'am – I cannot change for the worse.

[*Exit Lydia*
(I..ii.154–212)

DISCUSSION

All the books Lydia tells her maid to hide are novels and all the books she wants displayed around the room are books concerned with morality and religion, works aiming to teach their readers proper moral behaviour. In the eighteenth century novels enjoyed a bad reputation: they were not generally held to deserve the status of literature; many people in fact considered them to be bad from a moral point of view, leading to sinful thoughts and acts. Novels were deemed responsible for some young women's strange ideas about marriage and marital love, ideas such as the right to marry freely whom one chooses and the wish to marry for love instead of social position or money.

Eighteenth-century hairdressers required little pieces of paper to curl ladies' hair. The fact that Lydia's hairdresser has used the book of sermons, which is alphabetically organized, up to the letter 'P' means that more than half the book has been consumed in this way. This tells us how little regard Lydia has for this sort of book.

Lydia is clever and practical. She can quickly and successfully extricate herself from an incriminating situation. Her words present her to us as an intelligent, articulate, capable young woman. She does talk less than her aunt, her speeches are short – mainly because she is frequently interrupted by Mrs Malaprop – but she always speaks to the point. Her use of the words *preference* and *aversion* triggers her aunt's rage but they also encapsulate for us Lydia's views of marriage: her sentimental self-education through the reading of novels has taught her that she ought to choose her own husband and she will never marry someone she dislikes. Her replies to her aunt make clear how resolute she is.

THE EDUCATION OF YOUNG WOMEN

Both Sir Anthony and Mrs Malaprop are surprised and annoyed at Lydia's stubborn rejection of her aunt's suggestion that she should give up the man she loves and they blame it on her novel-reading. After Lydia's exit, Sir Anthony and Mrs Malaprop remain on stage and discuss how women should be brought up. Women's education, whether they ought to have any schooling and if yes, what they ought to be taught, was a topic very much in the air throughout the eighteenth century. Some people thought women should not be sent to school or tutors, others thought women should be taught a little so that they would not shame their husbands by proving total ignoramuses, but that there was no need to teach them a lot. Very few thought young women should have access to – and be encouraged to benefit from – the same education as that given to their brothers. There is, however, a clear sign that things are changing, because Sheridan uses Mrs Malaprop's and Sir Anthony's reactionary views on women's education to characterize them – and to make fun of them.

Read the passage below to see how the conversation between Mrs Malaprop and Sir Anthony continues and while you read bear in mind the following questions:

a) **What are Mrs Malaprop's and Sir Anthony's views on young ladies' education and behaviour? What are Sir Anthony's views on married life?**
b) **Why are they both comic and ridiculous characters?**
c) **Can you spot Mrs Malaprop's malapropisms? They are particularly amusing here, in the light of what she says. Why?**

> MRS MALAPROP: There's a little intricate hussy for you!
>
> SIR ANTHONY: It is not to be wondered at, Ma'am – all this is the natural consequence of teaching girls to read. Had I a thousand daughters, by heaven! I'd as soon have them taught the black art as their alphabet!
>
> MRS MALAPROP: Nay, nay, Sir Anthony, you are an absolute misanthropy!
>
> SIR ANTHONY: In my way hither, Mrs Malaprop, I observed your niece's maid coming forth from a circulating library! She had a book in each hand – they were half-bound volumes, with marble covers! From that moment I guessed how full of duty I should see her mistress!
>
> MRS MALAPROP: Those are vile places, indeed!
>
> SIR ANTHONY: Madam, a circulating library in a town is as an ever-green tree of diabolical knowledge! It blossoms through the year! And depend on it, Mrs Malaprop, that they who are so fond of handling the leaves, will long for the fruit at last.
>
> MRS MALAPROP: Well, but Sir Anthony, your wife, Lady Absolute, was fond of books.
>
> SIR ANTHONY: Aye – and injury sufficient they were to her, Madam. But were I to choose another helpmate, the extent of her erudition

should consist in her knowing her simple letters without their mischievous combinations; and the summit of her science be – her ability to count as far as twenty. The first, Mrs Malaprop, would enable her to work A.A. upon my linen; and the latter would be quite sufficient to prevent her giving me a shirt, No.1 and a stock, No.2.

MRS MALAPROP: Fie, fie, Sir Anthony, you surely speak laconically!

SIR ANTHONY: Why, Mrs Malaprop, in moderation, now, what would you have a woman know?

MRS MALAPROP: Observe me, Sir Anthony. I would by no means wish a daughter of mine to be a progeny of learning; I don't think so much learning becomes a young woman; for instance – I would never let her meddle with Greek, or Hebrew, or Algebra, or Simony, or Fluxions, or Paradoxes, or such inflammatory branches of learning – neither would it be necessary to her to handle any of your mathematical, astronomical, diabolical instruments. But, Sir Anthony, I would send her, at nine years old, to a boarding-school, in order to learn a little ingenuity and artifice. Then, Sir, she should have a supercilious knowledge in accounts; and as she grew up, I would have her instructed in geometry, that she might know something of the contagious countries; but above all, Sir Anthony, she should be mistress of orthodoxy, that she might not misspell, and mispronounce words so shamefully as girls usually do; and likewise that she might reprehend the true meaning of what she is saying. This, Sir Anthony, is what I would have a woman know; and I don't think there is a superstitious article in it.

(I.ii.213–61)

DISCUSSION

Sir Absolute's views on women's education exemplify the most reactionary, recalcitrant position on the issue: the less women know the better. He is comic because his speech is full of *hyperbole*: he says that women should not go beyond learning the individual letters of the alphabet and that there is no need for them to learn to read. His ideal wife is one who is illiterate and only distinguishes the letters sufficiently to be able to look after his linen. This is even more amusing if we remember that Mrs Malaprop has just said his late wife, Lady Absolute, was a learned woman who was fond of books.

hyperbole

Mrs Malaprop's views on what women should be taught are by no means radical, although she attempts to persuade Sir Anthony that a little learning does a woman good. The funny bit comes when we notice that Mrs Malaprop, the advocate of a little learning but not too much, makes all sorts of lexical mistakes which betray her own ignorance. She seems to think that serious science, mathematics, chemistry and astronomy should not be the concern of women, but women ought to know a little bit of arithmetics, a bit of geography and above all the spelling and meaning of the words they use. Her speech becomes highly amusing when we realise that she herself does not know at all the meaning of half the words she uses; she continually gets them wrong, unconsciously peppering her speech with frequent malapropisms. Here are a few examples from the end of her defence of women's need to be educated (the malapropisms are followed by the word she actually means between brackets and in italics):

but above all, Sir Anthony, she should be mistress of orthodoxy (*orthography*), that she might not misspell, and mispronounce words so shamefully as girls usually do; and likewise that she might reprehend (*apprehend*) the true meaning of what she is saying. This, Sir Anthony, is what I would have a woman know; and I don't think there is a superstitious (*superfluous*) article in it.

Mrs Malaprop herself is the best proof of the need of schooling that eighteenth-century women had, because she hardly apprehends the true meaning of the words she utters. She is a comic figure because she has such a distorted picture of herself, because she is the opposite of what she believes she is, because she should apply to herself what she preaches.

Despite their differences on the issue of women's education, Sir Anthony and Mrs Malaprop seem to share the same attitude towards marriage: young people should marry whoever they are told to marry; they should oblige their betters and let their husband or wife be chosen for them by their parents or relatives. Once married, women have no business but to please their husbands. They therefore agree on one point: that Lydia must give up all hopes of marrying Beverley and must marry instead Sir Anthony's son, Captain Absolute. But nobody knows that Beverley and Absolute are one and the same person, and this gives occasion for many comic scenes.

COMEDY AND THE CONFUSION OF IDENTITY

Mistaking one person for another and ignoring that those who are believed to be two different persons are in fact the same person are staple ingredients of comedy. They are already found in classical Greek comedies. The confusion of identity is exploited by Sheridan here to make us laugh and to make us think. We laugh at Mrs Malaprop's blunders and we think about what she means rather than what she actually says. We have to make up our minds whether we agree with her or whether we oppose the ideas she defends.

Read the first interview between Mrs Malaprop and Captain Absolute, which is reproduced below. Consider the following points:

a) **What are the ideological positions taken up by Mrs Malaprop here? Do you agree with any of them?**

b) Where does the comic appeal of this scene lie? Try to decode the *double entendre* of Absolute's speeches.

c) Towards the end of this passage Mrs Malaprop's malapropisms take a grammatical turn. Can you explain them?

MRS MALAPROP: Your being Sir Anthony's son, Captain, would itself be a sufficient accommodation; but from the ingenuity of your appearance, I am convinced you deserve the character here given of you.

ABSOLUTE: Permit me to say, Madam, that as I never yet have had the pleasure of seeing Miss Languish, my principal inducement in this affair at present, is the honour of being allied to Mrs Malaprop, of whose intellectual accomplishments, elegant manners, and unaffected learning, no tongue is silent.

MRS MALAPROP: Sir, you do me infinite honour! I beg, Captain, you'll be seated. [*They sit*] Ah! Few gentlemen, nowadays, know how to value the ineffectual qualities in a woman! Few think how a little knowledge becomes a gentlewoman! Men have no sense now but for the worthless flower of beauty!

ABSOLUTE: It is but too true indeed, Ma'am – yet I fear our ladies should share the blame – they think our admiration of beauty so great, that knowledge in them would be superfluous. Thus, like garden-trees, they seldom show fruit, till time has robbed them of the more specious blossom. Few, like Mrs Malaprop and the orange-tree, are rich in both at once!

MRS MALAPROP: Sir – you overpower me with good-breeding. He is the very pineapple of politeness! You are not ignorant, Captain, that this giddy girl has somehow contrived to fix her affections on a beggarly, strolling, eavesdropping Ensign, whom none of us have seen and nobody knows anything of.

ABSOLUTE: Oh, I have heard the silly affair before. I'm not at all prejudiced against her on that account.

MRS MALAPROP: You are very good, and very considerate, Captain. I am sure I have done everything in my power since I exploded the affair! Long ago I laid my positive conjunctions on her never to think on the fellow again – I have since laid Sir Anthony's preposition before her – but I'm sorry to say she seems resolved to decline every particle that I enjoin her.

(III.iii.1–37)

Mrs Malaprop's ideological position regarding women's cultivation **DISCUSSION** of their intellect and freedom to choose their own husband is that women's intellectual capacities deserve more attention than they often get and that women, and her niece in particular, ought to marry as they are told by their parents and relatives. There might be those who frown upon women's intellectual endeavours, but most of us will agree with Mrs Malaprop on the first issue and disagree with regard to the second. However, audiences are certainly bound to disagree with Mrs Malaprop on the point of her own intellectual capacities, of which she has a very high opinion.

double entendre

Some of the comic appeal of this scene arises from Absolute's remarks which present a *double entendre*: they can be read and interpreted differently by Mrs Malaprop and the audience. When Absolute says, 'I'm not at all prejudiced against her on that account', Mrs Malaprop may think him very good-natured and liberal-minded, but the audience knows that he cannot possibly object to Lydia's affection for the 'beggarly, strolling, eaves-dropping Ensign' whom he himself has been impersonating.

The different interpretations are possible because Mrs Malaprop does not know that Absolute and Beverley are the same person but the audience does, and because Mrs Malaprop has an idea of herself which is very different from the idea the audience has formed of her. Mrs Malaprop thinks of herself as a learned, well-read woman, whose capacities in this sense go unnoticed and underestimated in polite society. The audience, on the other hand, knows how ignorant she really is, how she mistakes one word for another all the time, how her supposed learning is merely a thin veneer. So when Absolute says that he hopes to have 'the honour of being allied to Mrs Malaprop, of whose intellectual accomplishments, elegant manners, and unaffected learning, no tongue is silent', the audience laughs first of all because they decode this as

irony

an *ironic* remark, that is, they know Absolute believes the opposite of what he says. Mrs Malaprop takes it literally, as she shows in her reply, and then the audience can laugh again at the distorted image she has of herself. So the author intends the meaning of Absolute's words to be decoded differently by the audience and by Mrs Malaprop: *ironically* – as a criticism – by the audience and *literally* – as a compliment – by Mrs Malaprop.

FOR DISCUSSION: The nature of comedy

In chapter 4, we asked you to think of the constitutive features of tragedy. We would now like you to identify the basic ingredients of comedy. The present chapter will have given you a head start, but try to add more features to your list by referring to other comedies you have read or are reading.

PROJECT WORK: GENDER AND IDENTITY CONFUSION IN SHAKESPEAREAN COMEDY

Playing with the confusion of identities has always been one of the resources of comedy: classical Greek drama made use of it and so did Shakespeare. In

Shakespeare's comedies, the confusion may arise from the existence of identical twins, as in *The Comedy of Errors*, but it can also originate in disguise and concealment. In many of his comedies, change of identity is linked to a temporary transformation of a character's gender. Transformation is, in fact, one of the staple ingredients of Shakespearean comedy, particularly in the form of having a female character dress as a member of the opposite sex. Cross-dressing occurs in quite a few plays, from the early comedies to the last plays, as in *The Two Gentlemen of Verona*, *As You Like It*, *Twelfth Night* or *Cymbeline*.

In these plays, the presence of heroines dressed in male attire raises many questions concerning the relation between gender and identity. If Rosalind in *As You Like It* becomes Ganymede, is she still Rosalind? To what extent is identity dependent on gender? What is identity then? And how can we define gender? You may find it difficult to reach satisfactory answers to these questions, but you could begin to envisage some possible answers by exploring the different motives which tempt Shakespearean heroines to hide their identity and take up a male disguise. You could also study how their male identity affects their relations with other men and women in the play, what advantages they gain when they impersonate a man and what the consequences of these temporary gender transformations are for the fabric of each comedy. Think about what difference it makes if these female roles involving a male disguise are played by actresses (like nowadays) or by boy-actors (as in Shakespeare's time). Bear in mind that gender relations have changed significantly since the Renaissance: for a sixteenth-century Englishwoman, a male costume could bring about the power to act and freedom to speak as a male.

PROJECT WORK: WOMEN'S EDUCATION IN THE EIGHTEENTH AND NINETEENTH CENTURIES

a) Sheridan's views on women's education are not very different from those of other eighteenth-century writers. You could easily collect opinions on this issue from many women writers of the period, from Lady Mary Wortley Montagu to Mary Wollstonecraft. In fact Wollstonecraft's famous *A Vindication of the Rights of Woman* (1792) is a vindication of women's education. It would be interesting to place the opinions of eighteenth-century women writers next to the opinions of some of the canonical male writers of the period, such as Jonathan Swift and Alexander Pope. Swift's views on women's education can be found in *Gulliver's Travels, A Voyage to Lilliput*, Chapter VI, and Pope's poems for Martha Blount also address the issue here and there.

b) Romantic and early Victorian fiction by women was also concerned with the controversial issue of women's education. Read chapter 7 of this Workbook, which introduces you to the work of Jane Austen. Austen addresses this issue in all her novels, but most directly perhaps in *Mansfield Park* (1814). The Brontë sisters, educated by their father in the deserted moors of Yorkshire and trained to become teachers, have also discussed education, particularly through the figure of the governess. Charlotte Brontë's *Jane Eyre* (1847) is the novel which comes to mind most readily, but *Agnes Grey* (1847), written by Anne Brontë, also deals with the problems surrounding education. You could examine and compare the views of these novelists concerning the *form* of education (how should women be taught: at school, by private tutors or governesses?), the *conditions* of education (what were schools like? what were the lives of women teachers like? what was the role of corporal punishment in education?) and the *content* of education (what should women be taught? should they be taught the same as men? should they be taught Latin and Greek or just a little bit of history and geography so that they do not embarrass their husband by proving totally ignorant in public?). Finally you could compare the views of Jane Austen, Charlotte Brontë and Anne Brontë with those of the eighteenth-century writers that you have studied in (a) above. Do they share the same views or do Austen and the Brontës go well beyond them?

PROJECT WORK: RESTORATION COMEDY AND MARRIAGE

Lydia's views on young women's right to choose their husbands freely are shared by the heroines of other English comedies. Restoration comedy offers an excellent opportunity to study late seventeenth-century attitudes to marriage. Get hold of several plays by Sir George Etherege (1634?–91?), William Wycherley (1640?–1716) and William Congreve (1670–1729) and see if you can glean out of them different attitudes to the life led by married couples. A good place to start is Congreve's *The Way of the World*, Act IV, Scene I, a scene in which Mirabell and Millamant, who are about to become husband and wife, set down their conditions and preferences for their future life together.

ACTIVITY: MALAPROPISMS

Use a dictionary to help you find and explain all of Mrs Malaprop's word confusions. Mrs Malaprop is not the only character in English literature to commit such comic blunders. Other famous examples include Dogberry in Shakespeare's *Much Ado About Nothing* and Mrs Slipslop in Henry Fielding's novel *Joseph Andrews* (1742). Here, just for your enjoyment, is a dialogue full of puns extracted from Lewis Carroll's *Alice in Wonderland* (1865), in which the Mock Turtle describes his school days to Alice:

> 'I only took the regular course.'
> 'What was that?'
> 'Reeling and Writhing, of course, to begin with; and then the different branches of Arithmetic – Ambition, Distraction, Uglification and Derision.'
> . . . .
> 'What else had you to learn?'

'Well, there was Mystery, – Mystery, ancient and modern, with Seaography: then Drawling – the Drawling-master was an old conger-eel, that used to come once a week: he taught us Drawling, Stretching, and Fainting in Coils.'

. . . .

'I never went to the Classical master: he taught Laughing and Grief, they used to say.'

. . . .

'And how many hours a day did you do lessons?'
'Ten the first day, nine the next, and so on.'
'What a curious plan!'
'That's the reason they're called lessons: because they lessen from day to day.'

(from chapter 9)

REFERENCES AND SUGGESTIONS FOR FURTHER READING

Sheridan's *The Rivals* is available in the New Mermaids series, edited by Elizabeth Duthie and published by A&C Black. If you want to find out more about Sheridan's comedies, a good starting-point would be Peter Davison's Casebook series volume *Sheridan: Comedies* (Macmillan, 1986). A brief but useful introduction to the status and nature of comedy is Moelwyn Merchant's *Comedy* (Methuen, 1972). For Shakespearean comedy, two good places to start are L.G. Salingar, *Shakespeare and the Traditions of Comedy* (Cambridge University Press, 1974) and Ruth Nevo, *Comic Transformation in Shakespeare* (Methuen, 1980). The issue of gender in Shakespeare has received a great deal of critical attention; some studies which you may find helpful to navigate these critical waters are Linda Bamber, *Comic Women, Tragic Men: A Study of Gender and Genre in Shakespeare* (University of California Press, 1982), Jean E. Howard, 'Crossdressing, the theatre and gender struggle in Early Modern England', in *Shakespeare Quarterly* 39 (1988: 418–40) and Lisa Jardine, *Still Harping on Daughters: Women and Drama in the Age of Shakespeare* (Harvester, 1983).

6

DEGENERATE APEMEN OR HEROIC DREAMERS?

On Cultural Stereotypes and Synge's *The Playboy of the Western World*

representation

otherness

We have already briefly introduced the concept of *representation* in chapters 3 and 4. Representation is being studied a lot in contemporary literary criticism, especially the representation of oppressed social groups. For example, feminists examine critically the representations of women in literature and popular culture, and study the ways in which images of women are constrained by language; and postcolonial critics are looking at how racial *others* are marginalized and discriminated against through negative ideological constructions.

These studies reveal how particular cultural or literary representations of specific groups of people are naturalized and conventionalized, and are fully integrated into the culture's common sense. As a result we do not question them any longer; we do not even notice them.

ideology

In fact, of course, these representations are not natural, not necessary in any way; on the contrary, they are historically constructed and highly *ideological*. There is therefore an urgent need to make people aware of the ideological nature of these representations and, if they have pernicious effects, of the possibility of constructing alternative – perhaps less pernicious – representations.

Typically, incompatible or contradictory representations co-exist within a particular culture, since they are produced by a society which is itself full of internal conflicts and contradictions. So it should not surprise us that cultural representations are being fought over, contested or subverted. The representations which emerge victorious tend to be reified and naturalized at least for a while, before being challenged again in their supremacy by alternative representations associated with new movements of social or cultural change. Like all other (verbal or visual) texts, literary texts can intervene in both these

reification

denaturalization

processes of *reification* and *denaturalization*; in simple terms, they can have the effect of either reinforcing stereotypes or breaking them up.

In order to illustrate these effects, we look at cultural representations of the Irish in Anglo-Irish literature at the beginning of the twentieth century.

In Victorian England, there were two main colonial stereotypes of the Irish: first, the Stage Irishman, Irish Paddy as a comic figure of fun and ridicule, designed to entertain the audiences of English theatres and music-halls; and secondly, an even more negative image of the Irish which is illustrated by the caricature from *Punch* reproduced below. It shows Britannia protecting Hibernia from an Irish anarchist. **Carefully examine this visual representation and discuss the nature of the stereotype that it embodies.**

COLONIAL STEREOTYPES AND THE NATIONALIST IMAGE

PUNCH, OR THE LONDON CHARIVARI.—October 29, 1881.

TWO FORCES.

Reproduced with permission of Punch Ltd.

DISCUSSION   The representation embodies a more dangerous and openly hostile form of racism than the Stage Irishman stereotype: it is the negative image of Paddy as an apeman, which depicts the Irish as racially inferior barbarians, in need of being civilized by the superior English race.

Irish Literary Revival

At the turn of the century, a time when nationalist feelings were on the rise in Ireland, these colonial stereotypes were being fought against and contested by Anglo-Irish writers. In a direct attack on the Stage Irishman stereotype, Lady Gregory asserted that the aim of the Irish Literary Revival was to 'show that Ireland is not the home of buffoonery and of easy sentiment, as it has been represented, but the home of an ancient idealism' (1913/1972: 20). These writers inverted the colonial stereotypes and substituted for them noble and heroic images of Ireland and the Irish. For example, in 1902, W.B. Yeats, the most famous proponent of the Irish Literary Revival, wrote a short play entitled *Cathleen ni Hoolihan*, in collaboration with Lady Gregory. In it, an old woman asks for the sacrifice of young Irishmen's lives in the fight to drive out the 'strangers' who have taken her 'four beautiful green fields' (1902/1974: 250). At the very end of the play, the father asks his son whether he saw the old woman:

PETER [*laying his hand on Patrick's arm*]: Did you see an old woman going down the path?
PATRICK: I did not; but I saw a young girl, and she had the walk of a queen.

(1902/1974: 256)

What do the old woman and the young queen represent, and who are the strangers?

DISCUSSION   The strangers are of course the English colonizers who occupy the four provinces of Ireland, Munster, Connaught, Leinster and Ulster, and the old woman is a symbolic figure representing oppressed Ireland. By the end of the play, the old woman has changed into a beautiful and proud young queen, the symbol of a new and independent, beautiful and proud nation.

When the play was first performed in Dublin, the role of Cathleen ni Hoolihan was acted by Maud Gonne, the beautiful revolutionary with whom Yeats was madly in love and about whom he wrote many of his best poems. But Maud Gonne rejected Yeats as a suitor and married a committed revolutionary, John MacBride, who in 1916 took part in the Easter Rising of the Irish nationalists. They took over the General Post Office in Dublin's O'Connell Street and proclaimed the independence of Ireland, but the rebellion was brutally put down by the English army and the main leaders, including MacBride, were executed.

Later on, Yeats wondered whether artistic representations – such as his playlet *Cathleen ni Hoolihan* – are not only passive reflections of society but can also actively contribute to alternative constructions of reality:

Did that play of mine send out
Certain men the English shot?

('The Man and the Echo' 1933/1973: 393)

FOR DISCUSSION

Would you tend to agree or disagree with Yeats? How do you see the connection between literature and reality? And what are the differences between literature and propaganda?

Yeats also wrote a poem about the Easter Rising, called 'Easter 1916', in which he tries to define his own rather ambivalent reaction to the rebels, combining admiration for their heroic dream with a fear that their single-mindedness may have blinded them. But he feels quite certain that the Stage Irishman stereotype has now been definitively left behind, the 'casual comedy' of an Ireland where 'motley' was worn has been changed, even John MacBride – who Yeats used to see as a 'drunken vainglorious lout' – has been transformed, and a 'terrible beauty is born', the heroic dream of an independent Ireland (1933/1973: 202–5).

The battle over the image of Ireland and the Irish was fought in particular over the representation of the Irish peasant, who was seen as the very essence of Irish identity. Playwrights such as Lady Gregory and J.M. Synge, though born into the ruling Ascendancy class, wrote plays about the poor peasants of the west of Ireland, who spent their lives cutting turf, gathering furze or going out fishing in their canvas curraghs. These peasants were exploited by absentee landlords and forced to pay heavy taxes and rents to bailiffs and rent-collectors. If they were unable to pay, they were evicted and their houses were burnt down.

HOW APEMAN PADDY WAS TRANSFIGURED BY THE DREAM, OR THE NEW PEASANT DRAMA

In their new kind of peasant drama, Lady Gregory and Synge focused on the poorest of these peasants, the social misfits, tinkers, beggars and tramps. They idealized these figures, being fascinated both by their inborn nobility and their linguistic vitality. They felt that, because these characters were least tainted by materialistic aspirations, they cherished in their souls the highest dreams, not so much heroic dreams of nationalism and political freedom, but *daemonic dreams* of self-fulfilment and individual liberation.

daemonic dream

The daemonic dream is the self which might exist if the individual were allowed complete instinctual gratification. But in society the dream is always repudiated by powerful, internalized norms of censorship, which ensure the stability and continuity of the social body. As a result, the original dream is materialized, perverted and corrupted. But in some individuals, especially those who are less fully integrated into the community or who have high imaginative powers, the dream is ineffectively repressed, so that it continues to play a major role in their lives even though they may not be fully conscious of it. And if they try to communicate their dream to others, they can only convey it by means of symbolic representations.

PROJECT WORK: THE AMERICAN DREAM

For the brief space of this project work, we leave Ireland for America and go back in time to 1620. The Pilgrim Fathers had left England in the Mayflower and settled in New England. They all shared a hope of finding freedom and happiness in their new country. This was the origin of the American Dream: the dream that the individual can find self-fulfilment in this land of unlimited opportunities. But just like the 'daemonic dream' discussed above, the American dream of self-fulfilment was soon perverted by materialistic concerns and turned into the American dream of (financial) success.

One of the most powerful symbolic expressions of the American dream is Jay Gatsby, the eponymous hero of F. Scott Fitzgerald's famous novel *The Great Gatsby* (1926). Though Gatsby realizes the American dream of success by turning from poor farmer's son into self-made millionaire, he ultimately fails. Show how both Gatsby's dream and he himself are destroyed by a contradiction inherent in the dream between vulgar materialism and high idealism.

SYNGE'S *THE PLAYBOY OF THE WESTERN WORLD* We now have sufficient background information to turn to the fiercely comic masterpiece of the Irish Literary Renaissance, John Millington Synge's *The Playboy of the Western World*. The playboy referred to in the title is an unpromising young man, Christy Mahon, whose father has always looked upon him as a 'dirty stuttering lout' and an 'ugly young streeler' (1907/1968: 205). Christy had a violent altercation with his father, in which he hit him on the head with a loy (a kind of spade) and left him for dead. He wanders along the roads of Ireland until he arrives at a village in Mayo, where the locals – including in particular Pegeen Mike, the publican's daughter – welcome and fête him as a hero, the noble and heroic slayer of his father. Delighted with this unexpected reception, Christy looks at himself in the mirror in a new and approving way:

Didn't I know rightly, I was handsome, though it was the divil's own mirror we had beyond, would twist a squint across an angel's brow; and I'll be growing fine from this day, the way I'll have a soft lovely skin on me and won't be the like of the clumsy young fellows do be ploughing all times in the earth and dung.

(1907/1968: 193)

Can you connect this with what we said above about the colonial stereotypes of the Irish and the transfiguring power of the dream?

Old Mahon's view of his son is a false, distorted image of Christy's **DISCUSSION** self, as distorting as the colonial stereotypes which turned the Irish into drunken idiots or simianized barbarians. The admiring girls, on the other hand, present Christy with a positive, noble and heroic image of his self. He lives up to this new image, grows in self-confidence and in poetry, and in the process becomes aware of previously repressed parts of his self. In other words, the girls act as catalysts who release heroic potentialities hidden deep inside himself.

However, when his father suddenly turns up in the village, the whole story of the patricide is revealed to be a lie: Christy had not actually killed, but only wounded his father. The villagers now reject this hero who is no longer a hero in their eyes and even Pegeen Mike, the girl Christy was hoping to marry, turns against him. Will the villagers' sudden hostility break Christy and force him back into the old restrictive roles and stereotypes? **Read the final scene of the play and evaluate Christy's reaction:**

CHRISTY *in low and intense voice*: Shut your yelling, for if you're after making a mighty man of me this day by the power of a lie, you're setting me now to think if it's a poor thing to be lonesome it's worse, maybe, go mixing with the fools of the earth.

. . . .

MAHON *grimly, loosening Christy*: My son and myself will be going our own way, and we'll have great times from this out telling stories of the villainy of Mayo, and the fools is here. *To Christy, who is freed.* Come on now.

CHRISTY: Go with you, is it? I will then, like a gallant captain with his heathen slave. Go on now and I'll see you from this day stewing my oatmeal and washing my spuds, for I'm master of all fights from now. *Pushing Mahon.* Go on, I'm saying.

MAHON: Is it me?

CHRISTY: Not a word out of you. Go on from this.

MAHON *walking out and looking back at Christy over his shoulder*: Glory be to God! *With a broad smile.* I am crazy again.

Goes.

CHRISTY: Ten thousand blessings upon all that's here, for you've turned me a likely gaffer in the end of all, the way I'll go romancing through a romping lifetime from this hour to the dawning of the Judgment Day.

He goes out.

MICHAEL: By the will of God, we'll have peace now for our drinks. Will you draw the porter, Pegeen?

SHAWN *going up to her*: It's a miracle Father Reilly can wed us in the end of all, and we'll have none to trouble us when his vicious bite is healed.

PEGEEN *hitting him a box on the ear*: Quit my sight. *Putting her shawl over her head and breaking out into wild lamentations*. Oh, my grief, I've lost him surely. I've lost the only Playboy of the Western World.

(1907/1968: 225, 229)

DISCUSSION   Christy finally takes up the dream and accepts it as his own; it is fully integrated into his self. No longer is it constructed for him by Pegeen and the other girls, but he now constructs his own dream, by and for himself. At the same time, he realizes that he must free himself from the inhibiting influence of the community. This seems to be an essential limitation: in order to realize his dream, the dreamer has to embrace social alienation and existential loneliness. As for the community, it is left destitute, with the less sensitive ones (Michael and Shawn) just carrying on as before and the more sensitive ones (Pegeen) feeling the full bitterness of the loss.

Synge's play laments the repressive attitude of the community towards its finer spirits. The village community rejects Christy, just as the Catholic middle classes had rejected the great nationalist leader Parnell or indeed, just as the narrow-minded Irish audiences rejected Synge's *Playboy* when it was first performed in 1907 in Dublin's new national theatre, the Abbey. The audience broke up, shocked and scandalized, at the word 'shifts' (underclothes; Christy talks about a 'drift of chosen females, standing in their shifts' 1907/1968: 226), and there were scenes of rioting in the theatre. Synge was accused of reviving the Stage Irishman stereotype, and his play was seen as a slur upon the virtues of Irish peasant womanhood and hence of Ireland itself.

FOR DISCUSSION

a) Consider whether or to what extent these accusations were justified.

b) Performing the play: Explain how as a theatre or film director you would direct the characters in the final scene reproduced above. Act out the scene if you are working in a group.

c) Does the work that you have done on point (b) in any way affect the conclusions that you reached under (a), either reinforcing or contradicting them?

The dreamers, whether they are lonely vagrants like Christy Mahon or great artists like J.M. Synge, tend to be rejected by their fellow human beings, by what Lady Gregory calls 'the little men' (1971: II, 332), who are 'little' because they have no great dreams. Lady Gregory here refers to the narrow-minded, materialistic middle classes, who not only lack greatness themselves, but also view greatness in others suspiciously and try to repress it. The Irish society had a particularly destructive attitude towards its finest spirits; Yeats, Lady Gregory and Synge were among the few great Irish writers who remained in Ireland. Throughout their lives, all three fought against, and suffered from, the intellectual vulgarity and cultural sterility of the middle classes.

THE ARTIST AS DREAMER

Yet they never gave up the fight. Yeats and Lady Gregory, in particular, fought for the realization of their dream in the world of reality and used their art as a weapon to that end. Accounts of such fights as the *Playboy* riots (briefly referred to above) or the battle with Dublin Castle over Shaw's *The Shewing-Up of Blanco Posnet* can be read in any history of the Abbey Theatre, including Lady Gregory's own *Our Irish Theatre*.

Ultimately their dreams aimed at creating a new Ireland, in the realization of which they would have found fulfilment. Unlike Christy Mahon's dream, their dream was thus turned both outwards – towards society – and inwards, combining aesthetic and artistic ideals with social and political ones. But, like Christy, they were disillusioned as the Irish, instead of building a new heroic nation, engaged in internecine warfare and eventually, in 1922, established a free state which turned out to be more repressive and reactionary than the colonial regime it displaced.

We conclude the chapter with a brief look at the connections between representation and reality, though considerations of space do not permit us more than a few hints concerning these extremely complex cognitive and cultural processes.

CONCLUSION

Recent research in cognitive science indicates that the information in our minds is stored in mental representations, sets of beliefs, assumptions and expectations about particular aspects of experience. For example, based on our experience of drinking in English pubs, we have a pub schema which includes information about ordering drinks at the bar, paying for them as soon as we get them, etc. These *schemata* help us to process the new situations that we encounter every day. But, precisely because of their schematic simplifications and overgeneralizations, many of them – such as English and Irish people's mental representations of each other or indeed of themselves – are likely to be full of stereotyped images and prejudiced beliefs.

cognitive schemata

At this stage, we should like to put forward a somewhat controversial claim, which we ask you to assess critically: namely, the major difference between literary and non-literary texts may well be that, whereas the latter tend to harden and reinforce the stereotypical

defamiliarization

elements contained within our mental schemata, the former have the opposite effect of breaking up their stereotypicality, making us look at aspects of reality in a new light, *defamiliarizing* the familiar or, in the more powerful words of Yeats' 'Easter 1916', breaking up the 'stone' of fixed and rigid beliefs that obstructs the 'living stream' (1933/1973: 204).

So perhaps Yeats was right, though not in any simplistic way, when he wondered whether his *Cathleen ni Hoolihan* could have contributed to the bringing about of the Easter Rising. By successfully embodying the new nationalist dream, it helped to break up the restrictive colonial stereotypes and to shape new mental attitudes. But, as we have seen, the danger of stereotypification is inherent in all representations: the nationalist image was soon in danger of becoming itself a restrictive stereotype. At this moment in history came Synge's *Playboy* with its complex portrayal of both the brutality and the poetry of Irish peasant life. Its non-stereotypical vision of Irishness broke up not only the colonial images but also the nationalist image. It was so new and shocking that it was misunderstood and rejected by most of Synge's contemporaries. And yet, without defamiliarizing dreams, without a constant renewal of their mental schemata, their lives ended up as bleak as the future that Pegeen envisages at the end of *The Playboy of the Western World*. Nor should we feel infinitely superior to Synge's contemporary audiences for, as Lady Gregory reminds us, our own lives, too, will 'grow clogged and dull with the weight of flesh and of clay' unless we manage to 'live by the shining of those scattered fragments of [the Image-Makers'] dreams' (1971: II, 297).

ACTIVITY: THE LANGUAGE OF *THE PLAYBOY OF THE WESTERN WORLD*

In his plays, Synge uses a dramatic idiom based partly on the literal translation of Irish Gaelic into English. Go through the extracts from *The Playboy* again and find constructions that seem strange because they might be based on Gaelic syntax. How effective is this language at creating a highly poetic and colourful, brutal and romantic world? Also consider the political implications of using a form of English (the colonizer's language) invaded by the structures of the Gaelic language (the language of the colonized).

PROJECT WORK: CULTURAL REPRESENTATIONS

In this project we should like you to look at representations of class, race or gender. For example, you could look at the representation of workers and capitalists in Dickens' *Hard Times* (see chapter 8), and compare with other Victorian novels such as Benjamin Disraeli's *Sybil, or: The Two Nations* (1845) or Elizabeth Gaskell's *North and South* (1855). You might investigate for instance to what extent, after the traumatic experience of the French revolution, the workers tended to be represented as a threatening mob rather than as individualized human beings. What are the most common metaphors (e.g. metaphors of flood or fire) used to depict this mob? To what extent do these metaphors express the fears and anxieties of the upper classes? Are upper-class characters presented as innately superior to the working-class characters? Are the latter being stereotyped as irrational or perhaps even immoral? In general, try to determine whether or to what extent the novelists that you are studying break through the class prejudices of their time and set up a new and non-stereotypical vision of the class system.

Another fascinating subject would be to explore the changing nature of racial representations: e.g. representations of the black slave, from Aphra Behn's *Oroonoko* (1688) via Harriet Beecher Stowe's *Uncle Tom's Cabin* (1852) to Toni Morrison's *Beloved* (1987). Alternatively, you might prefer to focus on gender issues and look at the representation of women in Jane Austen's *Emma* (chapter 7) or Jean Rhys' *Wide Sargasso Sea* (chapter 9). And again, you should focus on the ways in which these novelists break through racial or gender stereotypes.

REFERENCES AND SUGGESTIONS FOR FURTHER READING

Quotations from W.B. Yeats are taken from *Selected Plays* (Pan Books, 1974) and from *Collected Poems of W.B. Yeats* (Macmillan, 1933/1973). Quotes by Lady Gregory are from *Our Irish Theatre* (Colin Smythe, 1913/1972) and *The Collected Plays*, Vol. II (Colin Smythe, 1971). Quotes by Synge are from *The Plays and Poems of J.M. Synge*, edited by T.R. Henn (Methuen, 1968).

If you want to find out more about representations of Ireland and the Irish, you should read Declan Kiberd's excellent *Inventing Ireland: The Literature of the Modern Nation* (Jonathan Cape, 1995). It starts with a question, 'If God invented whiskey to prevent the Irish from ruling the world, then who invented Ireland?' and proceeds to answer that facetious question in memorable and high-quality chapters with such intriguing titles as 'J.M. Synge – Remembering the Future' or 'Protholics and Cathestants'. Also of interest is Terry Eagleton's *Heathcliff and the Great Hunger: Studies in Irish Culture* (Verso, 1995), which contains a particularly good section on Anglo-Irish novelists.

7

TALKING ABOUT THE WEATHER
Emma and the Social Web of Dialogue

Emma is a novel full of subtle thoughts hiding behind everyday situations and conversations which at first sight seem to have no importance at all. In the following passage from *Emma*, several people have been invited to dinner at Hartfield, Emma's house, and they are chatting in groups before moving into the dining-room. The party consists of Emma Woodhouse, Mr Woodhouse (Emma's father), Mr John Knightley (Emma's brother-in-law, married to her sister Isabella, who is not present), Mr Knightley (Mr John Knightley's elder brother), Mr and Mrs Weston (Mrs Weston was until her marriage Emma's governess), Mr and Mrs Elton, and Miss Jane Fairfax. Jane Austen chooses this moment, when her characters make 'polite conversation' and exchange casual remarks, in order to show us how they react differently to an apparently inconsequential piece of news: Miss Fairfax, a young lady who has been suffering from ill health, went to the post-office in the morning when it was raining. Most of the conversation deals with this trivial event and the major topic of conversation is that Miss Fairfax, who is recovering from a persistent cold, should not have been walking in the rain, not even for the sake of her mail. Comments will be of two kinds: reproofs for not looking after her health and suggestions for alternative arrangements so that in future she does not venture out to fetch her letters in defiance of rain.

This seemingly uninteresting incident offers an excellent occasion for Jane Austen to study different aspects of human nature and to add finishing touches to the characterization of some of the novel's central characters; it is also an occasion for Emma to confirm her suspicion that if Miss Fairfax ventures to go out when it is evidently going to rain, she must have much interest in those letters she hopes to have waiting for her at the post-office.

The day came, the party were punctually assembled, and Mr John Knightley seemed early to devote himself to the business of being agreeable. Instead of drawing his brother off to a window while they waited for dinner, he was talking to Miss Fairfax. Mrs. Elton, as elegant as lace and pearls could make her, he looked at in silence – wanting only to observe enough for Isabella's information – but Miss Fairfax was an old acquaintance and a quiet girl, and he could talk to her. He had met her before breakfast as he was returning from a walk with his little boys, when it had been just beginning to rain. It was natural to have some civil hopes on the subject, and he said,

'I hope you did not venture far, Miss Fairfax, this morning, or I am sure you must have been wet. – We scarcely got home in time. I hope you turned directly.'

'I went only to the post-office,' said she, 'and reached home before the rain was much. It is my daily errand. I always fetch the letters when I am here. It saves trouble, and is a something to get me out. A walk before breakfast does me good.'

'Not a walk in the rain, I should imagine.'

'No, but it did not absolutely rain when I set out.'

Mr. John Knightley smiled, and replied,

'That is to say, you chose to have your walk, for you were not six yards from your own door when I had the pleasure of meeting you; and Henry and John had seen more drops than they could count long before. The post-office has a great charm at one period of our lives. When you have lived to my age, you will begin to think letters are never worth going through the rain for.'

There was a little blush, and then this answer,

'I must not hope to be ever situated as you are, in the midst of every dearest connection, and therefore I cannot expect that simply growing older should make me indifferent about letters.'

'Indifferent! Oh! no – I never conceived you could become indifferent. Letters are no matter of indifference; they are generally a very positive curse.'

'You are speaking of letters of business; mine are letters of friendship.'

'I have often thought them the worst of the two,' replied he coolly. 'Business, you know, may bring money, but friendship hardly ever does.'

'Ah! you are not serious now. I know Mr John Knightley too well – I am very sure he understands the value of friendship as well as any body. I can easily believe that letters are very little to you, much less than to me, but it is not your being ten years older than myself which makes the difference, it is not age, but situation. You have every body dearest to you always at hand, I, probably, never shall again; and therefore till I have outlived all my affections, a post-office, I think, must always have power to draw me out, in worse weather than to-day.'

'When I talked of your being altered by time, by the progress of years,' said John Knightley, 'I meant to imply the change of situation which time usually brings. I consider one as including the other. Time will generally lessen the interest of every attachment not within the daily circle – but that is not the change I had in view for you. As an old friend, you will allow me to hope, Miss Fairfax, that ten years hence you may have as many concentrated objects as I have.'

It was kindly said, and very far from giving offence. A pleasant 'thank you' seemed meant to laugh it off, but a blush, a quivering lip, a tear in the eye, shewed that it was felt beyond a laugh. Her attention was now claimed by Mr Woodhouse, who being, according to his custom on such occasions, making the circle of his guests, and paying his particular compliments to the ladies, was ending with her – and with all his mildest urbanity, said,

'I am very sorry to hear, Miss Fairfax, of your being out this morning in the rain. Young ladies should take care of themselves. – Young ladies are delicate plants. They should take care of their health and their complexion. My dear, did you change your stockings?'

'Yes, sir, I did indeed; and I am very much obliged by your kind solicitude about me.'

'My dear Miss Fairfax, young ladies are very sure to be cared for. – I hope your good grandmamma and aunt are well. They are some of my very old friends. I wish my health allowed me to be a better neighbour. You do us a great deal of honour to-day, I am sure. My daughter and I are both highly sensible of your goodness, and have the greatest satisfaction in seeing you at Hartfield.'

The kind-hearted, polite old man might then sit down and feel that he had done his duty, and made every fair lady welcome and easy.

By this time, the walk in the rain had reached Mrs. Elton, and her remonstrances now opened upon Jane.

'My dear Jane, what is this I hear? – Going to the post-office in the rain! – This must not be, I assure you. – You sad girl, how could you do such a thing? – It is a sign I was not there to take care of you.'

Jane very patiently assured her that she had not caught any cold.

'Oh! do not tell me. You really are a very sad girl, and do not know how to take care of yourself. – To the post-office indeed! Mrs. Weston, did you ever hear the like? You and I must positively exert our authority.'

'My advice,' said Mrs Weston kindly and persuasively, 'I certainly do feel tempted to give. Miss Fairfax, you must not run such risks. – Liable as you have been to severe colds, indeed you ought to be particularly careful, especially at this time of year. The spring I always think requires more than common care. Better wait an hour or two, or even half a day for your letters, than run the risk of bringing on your cough again. Now do not you feel that you had? Yes, I am sure you are much too reasonable. You look as if you would not do such a thing again.'

'Oh! she shall not do such a thing again,' eagerly rejoined Mrs. Elton. 'We will not allow her to do such a thing again:' – and nodding significantly – 'there must be some arrangement made, there must indeed. I shall speak to Mr. E. The man who fetches our letters every morning (one of our men, I forget his name) shall inquire for your's too and bring them to you. That will obviate all difficulties you know;

and from us I really think, my dear Jane, you can have no scruple to accept such an accommodation.'

'You are extremely kind,' said Jane; 'but I cannot give up my early walk. I am advised to be out of doors as much as I can, I must walk somewhere, and the post-office is an object; and upon my word, I have scarcely ever had a bad morning before.'

'My dear Jane, say no more about it. The thing is determined, that is (laughing affectedly) as far as I can presume to determine any thing without the concurrence of my lord and master. You know, Mrs. Weston, you and I must be cautious how we express ourselves. But I do flatter myself, my dear Jane, that my influence is not entirely worn out. If I meet with no insuperable difficulties therefore, consider that point as settled.'

'Excuse me,' said Jane earnestly, 'I cannot by any means consent to such an arrangement, so needlessly troublesome to your servant. If the errand were not a pleasure to me, it could be done, as it always is when I am not here, by my grandmamma's.'

'Oh! my dear; but so much as Patty has to do! – And it is a kindness to employ our men.'

Jane looked as if she did not mean to be conquered; but instead of answering, she began speaking again to Mr. John Knightley.

. . . .

Jane's solicitude about fetching her own letters had not escaped Emma. She had heard and seen it all; and felt some curiosity to know whether the wet walk of this morning had produced any. She suspected that it had; that it would not have been so resolutely encountered but in full expectation of hearing from some one very dear, and that it had not been in vain. She thought there was an air of greater happiness than usual – a glow both of complexion and spirits.

She could have made an inquiry or two, as to the expedition and the expense of the Irish mails; – it was at her tongue's end – but she abstained. She was quite determined not to utter a word that should hurt Jane Fairfax's feelings; and they followed the other ladies out of the room, arm in arm, with an appearance of good-will highly becoming to the beauty and grace of each.

(*Emma*, Vol. II, Chapter XVI in O.U.P. edition; chapter 34 in Penguin ed.)

CHARACTERIZATION THROUGH DIALOGUE

The passage reproduced above mostly consists in a *tête-à-tête* between Mr John Knightley and Miss Fairfax, a private conversation which is interrupted with more or less delicacy and politeness by three other people: Mr Woodhouse, Mrs Elton, and Mrs Weston. It is significant that Mr Knightley and Emma are amongst the people present in the room who choose to remain silent while Miss Fairfax's walk in the rain is being discussed.

a) There are four people who scold Miss Jane Fairfax for walking to the post-office in the rain: Mr John Knightley, Mr Woodhouse, Mrs Elton and Mrs Weston, and they all do it differently. In what ways do they differ?
b) What do these different ways tell you about the characters themselves? Who is the most polite person and who is the most impolite one?
c) What are Jane Fairfax's reactions to the rebukes of these people? Are all her responses to these attempts to intrude into her life equally polite?

DISCUSSION   Although Mr John Knightley, Mr Woodhouse, Mrs Weston and Mrs Elton clearly manifest their disapproval of Jane Fairfax's walk in the rain and admonish her for the lack of concern she shows for her own health, the manner in which they do this differs greatly. Each of them selects a different approach, a different tactic, a different choice of words; as a result, some are more offensive, or less gentle, than others. These different ways of scolding Jane Fairfax expose different traits of personality, so that in the process of reproaching Miss Fairfax these four characters also reveal a great deal about themselves.

Mr John Knightley reproves Jane Fairfax but he does it gently. His admonishing in the end comes down to philosophically suggesting that when she grows up she will agree with him that one's health is more important than any letters: 'When you have lived to my age, you will begin to think letters are never worth going through the rain for.'

Mr Woodhouse scolds her indirectly and shows solicitude by asking her, as he would have asked his own daughter, if she changed her wet stockings: 'Young ladies are delicate plants. They should take care of their health and their complexion. My dear, did you change your stockings?' His comparison of young ladies to delicate plants implies that he thinks the health of young ladies is best preserved through inactivity but he never suggests that Miss Fairfax should give up her daily walk to the post-office. He suggests nothing which implies a privation of her freedom to go out whenever she pleases. He only recommends changing one's clothes if one gets wet.

Mrs Weston is rather more direct. Although she claims she is only offering advice, she is in fact rebuking Miss Fairfax: 'you must not run such risks', 'you ought to be particularly careful'. Mrs Weston addresses Jane Fairfax as she would have addressed, when she was a governess, one of the young people under her care. She addresses her firmly but with a touch of gentleness: 'Now do not you feel that you had? Yes, I am sure you are much too reasonable. You look as if you would not do such a thing again.' Her suggestion that next time Jane should wait for the rain to stop before going out for her daily errand to the post-office is a sensible piece of advice and does not curtail Jane's freedom to fetch her own letters. It only recommends putting it off.

Mrs Elton is the least indirect amongst them: she scolds Miss Fairfax loudly and openly. She treats her as a child who has done something wrong and is incapable of looking after herself. She is so self-centred that her rebuke is just as much about herself as about Jane Fairfax; Miss Fairfax got wet because *she*, Mrs Elton, was not with her to prevent it: 'You sad girl, how could you do such a thing? – It is a sign I was not there to take care of you.' This implies that if she had been there, she would have prevented Jane from getting wet by obstructing her freedom to go outdoors. In other words, Mrs Elton assumes that she is entitled to exert authority over Jane. Her impositions do not end here. Her offer to have one of her servants pick up Jane's mail is politely rejected by the latter the first time but Mrs Elton insists, to the point of becoming extremely impertinent. Her offer of help is cast in the mould of an order: 'Oh! she shall not do such a thing again. . . . We will not allow her to do such a thing again . . . there must be some arrangement made, there must indeed. I shall speak to Mr. E.' She is here taking the liberty of deciding what Jane will or will not do.

Each of these characters thus addresses Miss Fairfax in a different way. Mrs. Elton treats her as a silly girl who does not know what is good for her, Mrs Weston treats her as a child who has done something naughty, Mr Woodhouse equates her to a plant which can easily wither and ought to remain inactive, and only Mr John Knightley talks to her as an adult human being who has full possession of her free will and who consciously and knowingly chooses to do something that may have unwanted consequences, such as getting a bad cold, because she has reasons of her own to behave as she does.

Her reactions to the different proposals for future rainy mornings also vary in tone and content. She thanks Mr Woodhouse politely for showing concern for her health: 'Yes, sir, I did indeed; and I am very much obliged by your kind solicitude about me.' She accepts Mr John Knightley's gentle piece of admonishing, steering the conversation immediately afterwards into a different direction: 'I must not hope to be ever situated as you are, in the midst of every dearest connection, and therefore I cannot expect that simply growing older should make me indifferent about letters.' On the other hand, she has no chance to reply to Mrs Weston's advice because Mrs Elton abruptly intrudes into the conversation. She is, however, given a chance to respond to Mrs Elton's impolite offers. She does it gently at first, rejecting the offer because she needs the exercise that the walk to the post-office affords: 'You are extremely kind,' said Jane; 'but I cannot give up my early walk. I am advised to be out of doors as much as I can, I must walk somewhere, and the post-office is an object; and upon my word, I have scarcely ever had a bad morning before.' After Mrs Elton's second offensive, Miss Fairfax clearly states her refusal of the offer because if she chooses not to fetch the mail, there are servants in her household who can do the errand: 'Excuse me,' said Jane earnestly, 'I cannot by any means consent to such an arrangement, so needlessly troublesome to your servant. If the errand were not a pleasure to me, it could be done, as it always is when I am not here, by my grandmamma's.' After Mrs Elton's third attempt to press her offer further, Miss Fairfax decides to ignore her and her remarks altogether and resumes her conversation with Mr John Knightley: 'Jane looked as if she did not mean to be conquered; but instead of answering, she began speaking again to Mr. John Knightley.' So we see that Miss Fairfax replies to each of these people according to the way in which she is spoken to: with Mr John Knightley she behaves as an intelligent, educated young lady; to Mr Woodhouse she behaves as the polite acquaintance; and to Mrs Elton she behaves in an increasingly cold manner: correctly, but trying to put a stop to the intimacy Mrs Elton presumes exists between the two of them.

The differences in conversational behaviour displayed by these people enable the reader to obtain information to draw their **characterization** *characters*. Mr John Knightley comes across as a misanthrope who sees little need for cultivating human relations beyond the family circle but who, deep within, the reader guesses, is in fact an intelligent conversationalist who enjoys the presence of another human being when he is lucky enough to find the right company. Mr Woodhouse's comments on the delicate health of young ladies can be read as a gentle reproof of Miss Fairfax's behaviour and therefore present him as an extremely polite elderly gentleman who has a good command of a varied array of polite formulae for addressing ladies, showing concern about their health and enquiring about their relatives. He also comes across as a slightly silly old man too keen on giving advice about health matters, advice which in this case turns out to be simply a matter of common sense. Mrs Weston's kind rebuke is formulated with the persuasive strategies of a professional educator: her advice is framed with the rhetoric of a governess who knows that it is better to convince a child of the need to do something than to command imperiously and expect to be obeyed. She is firm, but she is also polite, the ideal picture of an English governess. By contrast with the other three, Mrs Elton's impertinence shines as an instance of sheer lack of manners. Her solicitude, by pressing her offers too far, becomes a display of her rudeness.

One thing to be noticed from the analysis of the conversational behaviour of these characters is that Jane Austen ridicules those who talk too much, and certainly those who talk when they are not supposed to. Mr Woodhouse interrupts the conversation Mr John Knightley and Miss Fairfax are having but, to a certain extent, he can be excused, since he is doing the circle of his guests, he is attending to his duties as a host. Mrs Elton has no such excuse: her behaviour in this scene seems to suggest, on Austen's part, a hatred of people who intrude into other people's conversations uninvited. In Austen's novels, characters who talk too much tend to be either downright stupid or socially pretentious. Mrs Elton is both: she is stupid enough to repeat twice an offer which has been rejected and she exposes herself to derision by behaving as if she had any ascendancy over Miss Fairfax, as if they were intimate or – as women would say in Jane Austen's time – 'particular' friends. It is clear that Miss Fairfax does not think this to be the case. On top of this, Mrs Elton's intention in offering to send one of her footmen to fetch Miss Fairfax's letters is clearly to display her social and economic status: to let everyone know that they have so many servants that they can spare one. She betrays her intention to show off when she declares that 'it is a kindness to employ our men', implying that there are so many of them that they remain idle most of the time. Her stupidity, lack of taste and social pretentiousness mix in her remarks about her husband, whom she affectedly calls 'Mr E.' and 'my lord and master': she first makes offers for which she then admits she requires her husband's consent and immediately afterwards she boasts she can persuade her husband of anything she takes a fancy to. Her display of wealth, feminine marital submission and feminine artful manipulation of domestic arrangements is entirely devoid of both taste and sense.

Two of the characters who refrain from meddling in the conversation, Mr Knightley and Emma, are amongst the ones Austen shows a greater regard for throughout the novel. It is also interesting that, by remaining silent, Emma and Mr Knightley offer two different viewpoints from which the reader can observe the scene: Emma listens with interest to the talk because she suspects that Miss Fairfax has something to hide, and the latter's trenchant defence of her right to fetch her letters seems to confirm it. Readers of the novel, even if they are reading it for the first time, can share Emma's viewpoint to a certain extent, because they do know Miss Fairfax has reasons to conceal the name of the person she corresponds with. So reading this scene from Emma's silent angle of observation, the reader is entangled in the mesh of intrigue created by the plot of *Emma*.

Mr Knightley's viewpoint, as a silent observer, would necessarily be different from Emma's. His concern for his brother's welfare would make him resent the intrusion of Mrs Elton in a conversation his brother seems to be enjoying; readers of the novel can imagine what Mr Knightley must think of a woman who takes the freedom of addressing him familiarly as 'Knightley'. For Mr Knightley and for the readers too, this scene confirms their worst suspicions about Mrs Elton's 'loudness': her rudeness masquerading as solicitude, her stupidity presenting itself as ingenuity, her offers of help as an occasion for vulgar display.

NARRATIVE
TECHNIQUE
AND POINT OF
VIEW

In Jane Austen's narrative technique, one sometimes comes across stretches of narrative text without dialogue in which one cannot be sure if the 'voice' which narrates is reporting what the narrator thinks or what a character in the novel thinks. There is a blurring of the boundaries which separate the narrator's point of view from the consciousness of a particular character. There is an example of this in the first paragraph of the passage from *Emma* quoted above. This initial paragraph is reproduced again here:

The day came, the party were punctually assembled, and Mr John Knightley seemed early to devote himself to the business of being agreeable. Instead of drawing his brother off to a window while they waited for dinner, he was talking to Miss Fairfax. Mrs. Elton, as elegant as lace and pearls could make her, he looked at in silence – wanting only to observe enough for Isabella's information – but Miss Fairfax was an old acquaintance and a quiet girl, and he could talk to her. He had met her before breakfast as he was returning from a walk with his little boys, when it had been just beginning to rain. It was natural to have some civil hopes on the subject, and he said . . .

Comment on the blending, the fusion, between the narrator's voice and the thinking of either Emma or Mr John Knightley in this paragraph. Can you spot any sentences, phrases, bits of text which sound as if spoken by the narrator and others which sound as if thought by a middle-aged man who is about to address a young woman?

DISCUSSION

voice

Paying attention to the point of view, to the 'angle of telling' from which a text is written, is always a rewarding exercise. Sometimes this can be difficult to do, because there are moments when one cannot be sure if one is listening to the *voice* of the narrator or the *voice* of a character. In the above extract, one can see this blending, this fusion between the narrator's voice and the thinking of either Emma or Mr John Knightley. Some of the sentences and phrases sound as if spoken by a narrator: 'The day came, the party were punctually assembled, and Mr John Knightley seemed early to devote himself to the business of being agreeable. Instead of drawing his brother off to a window while they waited for dinner, he was talking to Miss Fairfax.' This sounds like Jane Austen the narrator amusing herself by giving a picture of predictable behaviour in a character who has a not very pleasing or polite habit: to ignore the company and talk to his brother. However, the way Jane Austen has phrased it ('seemed early to devote himself to the business of being agreeable' and 'Instead of drawing his brother off to a window while they waited for dinner') suggests that Jane Austen the narrator is here seeing Mr John Knightley through the eyes of Emma: this far into the novel, the reader knows that this comment fits in very well with what Emma thinks of her sister's husband. The reader also knows that this is the kind of ironic comment Emma's wit could have prompted her to make to herself (or, indeed, to others, if given a chance). The fusion of the narrator's voice with Emma's consciousness is a frequent feature of this novel: many critics have noticed how much of the charm of *Emma* lies in its narrating much of what has to be narrated through Emma's consciousness.

There are, however, other sentences which do not seem to be conveying either the narrator's thoughts or Emma's voice but rather seem to be reproducing Mr John Knightley's thoughts. This is the case of one sentence in the passage above which can be seen as reproducing the train of thought of a married man attending a party without his wife, a married man who is about to address a younger woman whom he has known for a long while: 'Mrs. Elton, as elegant as lace and pearls could make her, he looked at in silence – wanting only to observe enough for Isabella's information – but Miss Fairfax was an old acquaintance and a quiet girl, and he could talk to her.' Describing Mrs Elton as being 'as elegant as lace and pearls could make her' is not a very charitable thing to do: it implies that Mrs Elton is not elegant at all, except for the lace and pearls she is wearing. So her elegance is not hers: it is something put on, phoney, bought with money. This thought could be attributed to both Jane Austen and John Knightley, since it would be concordant with other comments they have made in the novel. Initially we may feel that it still sounds like the voice of the narrator but when we are told that John Knightley is looking at her to collect information for his wife, we begin to wonder if we should also attribute to John Knightley the thought of Mrs Elton not being very elegant at all, except for her lace and pearls. By the time we get to 'Miss Fairfax was an old acquaintance and a quiet girl, and he could talk to her', it is easier to be persuaded that these are the very words Emma's brother-in-law would use to describe Miss Fairfax. If we conclude they are, then Jane Austen is using here one of the categories established by those critics who have studied the mechanics of speech and thought presentation in narrative. This technique, which we will discuss in much greater **free indirect** detail in chapter 10, is often referred to as *free indirect thought*.   **thought**

Jane Austen's 'little bit (two inches wide) of Ivory' is often packed with interesting thoughts and ideas. The incident about the post-office and the rain is in fact an excuse to have Mr John Knightley and Miss Jane Fairfax, two sensible, intelligent people, share a conversation which is both witty and profound. **DIALOGUE AND WIT**

a) If the trip to the post-office is just an excuse, what is their conversation really about?

b) Do you see any traces of wit, humour, irony in this dialogue?

DISCUSSION

Mr John Knightley and Miss Fairfax do in fact talk very little about the walk in the rain and the fetching of letters from the post-office. This incident simply provides the opening gambit for their conversation, an entertaining game of chess which they play while they wait to be summoned to the dining-room. Their conversation is about the use of letters, their good and bad points, about the advantages of having one's relations living near oneself, about the need to have what Emma herself has called, earlier in the novel, 'objects for the affections'. Mr John Knightley argues that letters are either a pest if they are business letters or thoroughly useless if they are letters of friendship. He sees no point in friendship, nor in any emotional attachment beyond 'the daily circle'. Miss Fairfax disagrees and stresses the importance of both letters and friends beyond one's immediate circle. He believes one is interested in letters when one is young and this interest grows smaller and smaller with time. She disagrees again and sees no relation between age and letters: one will always remain interested in letters if the people one loves and cares for do not live nearby.

All this exposition of contrary opinions is conducted not only in a very polite, serene mood, but also with a measure of wit and humour. On two occasions, Mr John Knightley's answers to Miss Fairfax take the shape of jests:

'I must not hope to be ever situated as you are, in the midst of every dearest connection, and therefore I cannot expect that simply growing older should make me indifferent about letters.'

'Indifferent! Oh! no – I never conceived you could become indifferent. *Letters are no matter of indifference; they are generally a very positive curse.*'

'You are speaking of letters of business; mine are letters of friendship.'

'*I have often thought them the worst of the two,*' replied he coolly. '*Business, you know, may bring money, but friendship hardly ever does.*'

wit

The italicized sentences contain two instances of Mr John Knightley's witticisms: as often in Jane Austen's fiction, *wit* and humour rely on a technique which consists in defeating the expectations of the reader. When he affirms that letters are not a matter of indifference (a negative quality), this affirmation raises the expectation of letters being a matter of something that is a positive quality. This expectation is totally contravened when he says that letters are a dreadful 'curse' (a quality even more negative than indifference). Wit – and sometimes humour too – rests on the capacity to take us by surprise.

Mr John Knightley's second jest is more ironic than witty. He seems to take delight in presenting himself as a man who dislikes company and the society of his fellow human beings: he sees no point in friendship, since it does not bring any profit. But is this really what he thinks? His eagerness to engage Miss Fairfax in conversation, as the reader is told at the beginning of this passage ('Miss Fairfax was an old acquaintance and a quiet girl, and he could talk to her'), seems to suggest that he does not totally recoil from the benefits of friendship and that his remark about friendship could be taken to be ironic.

The purpose of this chapter has been to show how what we call a 'character' in a novel is a complex entity which is created out of what the character says, what the narrator says about the character and what characters say, think and observe about each other. Information about a character can be conveyed through either narrative passages or dialogue. When it is conveyed through a dialogue in which the character speaks the reader has first-hand information about the character, information that is only mediated through the reader's own interpretative processes. When information is filtered through the narrator or through what a character says or thinks about another, the reader has to be alert and decide to what extent this information is reliable, to what extent this information is tinted with the perceptions of other 'voices'. This is what makes the process of reading a novel interesting and this is what enables a writer to achieve the variety in the representation of human nature which Jane Austen achieves in this apparently insignificant conversation from *Emma*. What Jane Austen does in this passage from *Emma* is to give us precisely what good novels are supposed to give their readers, according to her own defence of the novel at the end of Chapter 5 of *Northanger Abbey*: 'the most thorough knowledge of human nature, the happiest delineation of its varieties, the liveliest effusions of wit and humour . . . conveyed to the world in the best-chosen language.'

PROJECT WORK: *EMMA* AND CONVERSATIONAL STRATEGIES

In *Emma*, Vol. I, Chapter V, Mrs Weston and Mr Knightley have an interesting conversation in which they disagree about what is good and what is bad for Emma. Try to analyse their conversation using the present chapter as a model. Notice in particular how they politely disagree with each other and how each tries to redirect the topic of conversation to suit themselves.

PROJECT WORK: CHARACTERIZATION AND POINT OF VIEW IN *PERSUASION*

Chapter 20 in *Persuasion*, another of Jane Austen's novels, offers an opportunity to study the fusion of the voice of the narrator and the heroine's consciousness: read the chapter closely and see if you can identify those places in which the fusion takes place. (Before embarking on your analysis, it might be helpful to read chapter 10 of this Workbook, where you will find a more detailed discussion of these matters of point of view and characterization.)

The same chapter, Chapter 20 in *Persuasion*, can also be used to study how a character's personality is built through dialogue: some of the novel's characters appear here as either silly or socially pretentious. Jane Austen had a certain regard for witty people, but she could mercilessly crucify those characters she considered to be stupid. If besides being stupid the character was also socially pretentious, Austen would know no pity and would heartlessly expose such characters through their own stupid and snobbish talk, as she does with Mrs Elton in the passage discussed in this chapter. In order to draw her characters, Austen often makes use of what Gary Kelly (1989: 120) has called the *axis of volubility* (characters who talk a lot without much purpose are generally stupid) and the *axis of conventionality* (characters who constantly resort to clichés and catch-phrases are on the whole superficial, trivial, shallow and often, not to be trusted, insincere). Using Kelly's notions, explore how we can assign some of the characters who appear in *Persuasion*, Chapter 20 to either of these axes (or to both) with the help of the words they themselves speak in dialogue.

PROJECT WORK: JANE AUSTEN AND FEMINISM

Are Jane Austen's heroines – such as for instance Emma Woodhouse – intelligent and independent women whose marriages at the (happy-)end of the novels are based upon an equality of the sexes? Or do we have to interpret their marrying as a conservative move, a return within the patriarchal boundaries of society? How do you ultimately see Jane Austen herself: as a conservative thinker, as a radical proto-feminist, or perhaps a mixture of both?

When you think about these questions, do not forget to take into consideration the historical context in which Jane Austen lived: *Emma*, for example, was published in 1816, and in fact Jane Austen wrote most of her novels under the increasingly repressive and autocratic regime that Shelley attacked so bitterly in his 'Sonnet to England in 1819' (see p. 36).

The standard scholarly edition of Jane Austen's novels has been edited by R.W. Chapman, *The Works of Jane Austen* (Oxford University Press, 1954), and two of the most interesting biographies are Park Honan, *Jane Austen: Her Life* (Fawcett Columbine, 1987) and David Nokes, *Jane Austen: A Life* (Fourth Estate, 1997). 'The little bit (two inches wide) of Ivory on which I work with so fine a brush, as to produce little effect, after much labour' is a quotation from a letter Jane Austen wrote to her brother Edward.

Gary Kelly's chapter '"Only a Novel": Jane Austen', in *English Fiction of the Romantic Period 1789–1830* (Longman, 1989: 111–38) explains the concepts of axis of volubility and axis of conventionality and is a good introduction to the study of her novels. Other books which ought to be consulted for a study of Austen's novels are Marilyn Butler, *Jane Austen and the War of Ideas* (Clarendon Press, 1987), Alistair Duckworth, *The Improvement of the Estate: A Study of Jane Austen's Novels* (Johns Hopkins University Press, 1971), Mary Poovey, *The Proper Lady and the Woman Writer: Ideology as Style in the Works of Mary Wollstonecraft, Mary Shelley and Jane Austen* (University of Chicago Press, 1984) and Deborah Kaplan, *Jane Austen Among Women* (Johns Hopkins University Press, 1992).

REFERENCES AND SUGGESTIONS FOR FURTHER READING

8

OF ELEPHANTS, SERPENTS AND FAIRY PALACES

Simile and Metaphor in Dickens' *Hard Times*

Compare the following two sentences:

My friend James is like an elephant.
My friend James is an elephant.

simile

metaphor

ground of the comparison

The first sentence contains a *simile*, with the word 'like' making explicit the comparison between 'my friend James' and 'an elephant'. The second sentence contains a *metaphor*: 'like' has been dropped, and the sentence sets up a relation of identity between the two terms, at least with respect to one or more particular features.

The features that are shared by James and elephants are usually referred to as the *ground of the comparison*. It is important to make this ground as explicit as possible, but even with a simple comparison like that between James and an elephant it can be indeterminate and context-dependent. For example, our comparison might suggest any of the following grounds in various contexts:

My friend James is as large as an elephant.
He has as good a memory as an elephant.
He is as thick-skinned as an elephant.
He is as clumsy as an elephant.

This is of course why similes and metaphors are such effective rhetorical devices and why they are so highly valued by writers: they can suggest to readers a wide array of interpretive directions.

Similes and metaphors range from simple and hackneyed comparisons such as the one discussed above to highly original and creative ones, which are perhaps more typical of literary or even poetic discourse. Let us turn to an example from Shakespeare in order to illustrate the latter. Towards the end of *Macbeth*, the eponymous hero reflects about the meaning of life in general and his life in particular. Relying on one of the metaphors that Macbeth uses in the soliloquy quoted below, we could say that in his own life he had acted poorly (or badly) when he killed King Duncan and became a dictator steeped in blood. As a result of this cruel deed, his life has lost all meaning:

> Life's but a walking shadow, a poor player
> That struts and frets his hour upon the stage,
> And then is heard no more: it is a tale
> Told by an idiot, full of sound and fury,
> Signifying nothing.
>
> (V.v.5, 24–8)

GLOSSARY

but only
player actor
to strut to walk in a proud way
to fret to speak in a passionate way

Examine the metaphors that Macbeth uses in these lines to describe life and try to specify the ground for each metaphor. What do these metaphors tell us about Macbeth's view of life at this stage of the play?

For Macbeth, life has become something unreal or insubstantial (a shadow), something that cannot be taken seriously and that evokes in us a feeling of pity rather than admiration (a *poor* or incompetent player, whose acting is mere strutting and fretting). Moreover, life is transient or even ephemeral (the actor struts and frets *his* hour upon the stage,/ And then *is heard no more*); and behind the outward show of 'sound and fury', it is ultimately absurd and futile (a tale/ Told by an idiot . . . / Signifying nothing). **DISCUSSION**

Metaphors are common not only in poetry or poetic drama but in most text-types, and we devote the remainder of this chapter to an analysis of metaphors in a literary prose text, Charles Dickens' novel *Hard Times*.

In 1854 Charles Dickens went to Preston during the 23-week strike of **HARD TIMES**
the cotton-mill workers in order to gather material for *Hard Times*. Here are his impressions of Preston, which in the novel is called Coketown:

Coketown, to which Messrs Bounderby and Gradgrind now walked, was a triumph of fact; it had no greater taint of fancy in it than Mrs Gradgrind herself. Let us strike the key-note, Coketown, before pursuing our tune.

It was a town of red brick, or of brick that would have been red if the smoke and ashes had allowed it; but, as matters stood it was a town of unnatural red and black like the painted face of a savage. It was a town of machinery and tall chimneys, out of which interminable serpents of smoke trailed themselves for ever and ever, and never got uncoiled. It had a black canal in it, and a river that ran purple with ill-smelling dye, and vast piles of buildings full of windows where there was a rattling and a trembling all day long, and where the piston of the steam-engine worked monotonously up and down, like the head of an elephant in a state of melancholy madness.

(65)

Study the similes and metaphors in the second paragraph and discuss their implications.

DISCUSSION

In an interesting simile, the town with its unnatural colours of red and black is compared to 'the painted face of a savage'. 'Unnatural' applies not only to the colours but also to the inhabitants of the town who are forced to live in an 'unnatural' state of *alienation*

alienation

brought about by the soul-numbing horror of the industrial environment. Moreover 'savage' suggests that, as a result of this unnatural repression and distortion of their true selves, a savage force has built up inside the people, which could erupt at any time.

In another simile, the pistons of the steam-machines are compared to the heads of elephants in a state of melancholy madness. It evokes a mechanical world of never-ending repetition which benumbs people, destroys their joy and vitality, and reduces them to a state of madness and despair.

The image of the 'serpents of smoke' is a metaphor rather than a simile, since there is no word such as *like* which makes the comparison explicit. Among other suggestions such as danger or disgust, this metaphor evokes the Biblical story of the serpent in Paradise who corrupts mankind, thus implying that there is an element of evil in the squalid mechanical world of Coketown.

Now compare the above passage with the following extracts which occur a bit later in the novel and consider how we can describe Dickens' technique:

[1] The lights in the great factories, which looked, when they were illuminated, like Fairy palaces – or the travellers by express train said so – were all extinguished; and the bells had rung for knocking off for the night, and had ceased again; and the Hands, men and women, boy and girl, were clattering home.

(103)

[2] The Fairy palaces burst into illumination, before pale morning showed the monstrous serpents of smoke trailing themselves over

Coketown. A clattering of clogs over the pavement; a rapid ringing of bells; and all the melancholy-mad elephants, polished and oiled up for the day's monotony, were at their heavy exercise again.

(107)

[3] They were now in the black by-road near the place, and the Hands were crowding in. The bell was ringing, and the Serpent was a Serpent of many coils, and the Elephant was getting ready.

(117)

DISCUSSION What happens almost each time is that Dickens starts with a simile which makes the comparison explicit (piston of the steam-engine like the head of an elephant; factories like Fairy palaces); then, on the second occasion of use, he relies on his readers' memory and does not bother to spell out the comparison again. In other words, the similes have been turned into metaphors (passage 2). Finally, in the last passage, he uses a condensed version of the metaphors, simply referring to *the Serpent* and *the Elephant*, and expecting his readers to be able to retrieve the intended referents (the columns of smoke and the machines).

Finally, consider also the implications of these metaphors and how they contrast with the metaphor used to describe the workers in passages (1) and (3).

DISCUSSION animistic metaphors Dickens develops an ironic contrast by describing the mechanical world in terms of highly imaginative metaphors (e.g. factories as Fairy palaces) and in particular *animistic metaphors* (the smoke and the machines as animate beings, respectively serpents and elephants), whereas the workers are described in terms of a *de-humanizing metaphor* (the Hands), which reduces them to the status of mere tools. **dehumanizing metaphors**

GRADGRIND After the Hands, let us now turn to the ideologically potent description of the masters and, first of all, Mr Gradgrind. He is introduced in the very first chapter of the novel:

'Now, what I want is, Facts. Teach these boys and girls nothing but Facts. Facts alone are wanted in life. Plant nothing else, and root out everything else. You can only form the minds of reasoning animals upon Facts: nothing else will ever be of any service to them. This is the principle on which I bring up my own children, and this is the principle on which I bring up these children. Stick to Facts, sir.'
    The scene was a plain, bare, monotonous vault of a schoolroom, and the speaker's square forefinger emphasized his observations by underscoring every sentence with a line on the schoolmaster's sleeve. The emphasis was helped by the speaker's square wall of a forehead,

which had his eyebrows for its base, while his eyes found commodious cellarage in two dark caves, overshadowed by the wall. The emphasis was helped by the speaker's mouth, which was wide, thin, and hard set. The emphasis was helped by the speaker's voice, which was inflexible, dry, and dictatorial. The emphasis was helped by the speaker's hair, which bristled on the skirts of his bald head, a plantation of firs to keep the wind from its shining surface, all covered with knobs, like the crust of a plum pie, as if the head had scarcely warehouse-room for the hard facts stored inside. The speaker's obstinate carriage, square coat, square legs, square shoulders – nay, his very neckcloth, trained to take him by the throat with an unaccommodating grasp, like a stubborn fact, as it was – all helped the emphasis.

'In this life, we want nothing but Facts, sir; nothing but Facts!'

The speaker, and the schoolmaster, and the third grown person present, all backed a little, and swept with their eyes the inclined plane of little vessels then and there arranged in order, ready to have imperial gallons of facts poured into them until they were full to the brim.

(47–8)

a) **Discuss Gradgrind's view of education. (Compare this with the Pink Floyd video 'Hey Teacher, Leave Those Kids Alone' from *The Wall* if you happen to have a copy of it.) What would be your ideal system of education and what effect should it have on the children who undergo it? By way of contrast, look at the last sentence of the Dickens passage and consider the effect that Gradgrind's system of education has on the Coketown children.**

b) **Analyse in detail the grotesque metaphors that Dickens uses in the second paragraph in order to describe Gradgrind. Find out in particular what the following are compared to:**

Gradgrind's forehead = ?
his eyes = ?
the few hairs on his head = ?
the top of his head = ?
the inside of his head = ?

As usual, you should also think about the thematic and ideological implications of these metaphors.

DISCUSSION

a) Just like the workers, the children are described in terms of a dehumanizing metaphor: they are reduced to 'vessels' or containers which are to be filled full of facts. The system seems to have this deadening effect on all the people upon whom it is imposed, whether it is the workers who are enslaved to the machines or the children who are subjected to a purely *utilitarian*

utilitarianism   education.

b) The answers are as follows:

> forehead = wall of a building
> eyeholes = cellar (two caves)
> hairs = fir trees
> surface of head = knobbly crust of a plum pie
> inside of head = warehouse overflowing with facts

These similes and metaphors make Gradgrind look like a grotesque monster, whose 'square' world of fact exerts a restrictive and imprisoning effect upon everybody including himself. The impression of a world of constriction is reinforced by the image of the neckcloth taking him 'by the throat with an unaccommodating grasp' in the last sentence of this paragraph.

The grotesque metaphors used to describe Gradgrind's head and hair suggest that he lives in a world of constriction and repression.

METAPHORS OF HAIR

Compare this with the equally potent descriptions of the hair of the other main characters in the story. What do they suggest about the worlds that these characters inhabit?

a) Mr Bounderby, the other capitalist:

He had not much hair. One might have fancied he had talked it off; and that what was left, all standing up in disorder, was in that condition from being constantly blown about by his windy boastfulness.

(59)

(b) the two representatives of the working class, Stephen and Rachael:

A rather stooping man, with a knitted brow, a pondering expression of face, and a hard-looking head sufficiently capacious, on which his iron-grey hair lay long and thin, . . .

(103)

She turned, being then in the brightness of a lamp; and raising her hood a little, showed a quiet oval face, dark and rather delicate, irradiated by a pair of very gentle eyes, and further set off by the perfect order of her shining black hair.

(104)

(c) two of the children, the model pupil Bitzer and the circus girl Sissy:

The square finger, moving here and there, lighted suddenly on Bitzer, perhaps because he chanced to sit in the same ray of sunlight which, darting in at one of the bare windows of the intensely white-washed room, irradiated Sissy. . . . But, whereas the girl was so dark-eyed and dark-haired, that she seemed to receive a deeper and more lustrous colour from the sun when it shone upon her, the boy was so light-eyed and light-haired that the self-same rays appeared to draw out of him what little colour he ever possessed.

(49–50)

DISCUSSION

a) Bounderby, the other representative of the world of fact, differs from Gradgrind in that his world is not one of constriction, but rather one of turbulence, of chaos and 'disorder', which is caused by his constantly boasting about how he rose from destitute street urchin to powerful industrialist – a typical narrative of the self-made capitalist, which later on in the novel is revealed to be nothing but a tissue of lies.

b) Note the contrasts between Gradgrind's warehouse head overflowing with facts and Stephen's 'sufficiently capacious' head, and also between Bounderby's dishevelled and Stephen's well-ordered hair. The idea of order associated with Stephen and Rachael's world is made explicit in the description of the latter: 'the perfect order of her shining black hair'. Order is here combined with emotions and natural affections (her 'very gentle eyes') to bring about a 'perfect' world of moral awareness and genuine feelings.

c) Finally, the contrast between Sissy and Bitzer, between the circus girl and the model pupil, is that between the vitality of a warm-hearted human being and the rigidity of an emotionless robot; in short, it is the contrast between life and death.

So we can graphically represent the basic oppositions in *Hard Times* as follows:

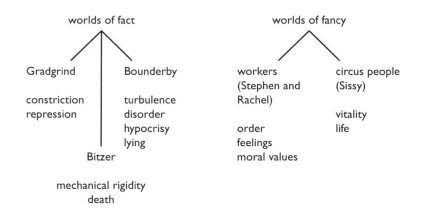

worlds of fact

Gradgrind   Bounderby

constriction   turbulence
repression   disorder
                   hypocrisy
                   lying
         Bitzer

mechanical rigidity
death

worlds of fancy

workers   circus people
(Stephen and   (Sissy)
Rachel)
                   vitality
order   life
feelings
moral values

There is a problem, however, with Dickens' fact–fancy distinction, and this is an ambiguity in his use of the word *fancy*. At times he uses it in the sense of feelings, but in other passages he uses it in the sense of imagination. Fancy in the sense of feelings is indeed associated with Stephen and Rachael (as in passage b above), but fancy in the sense of imagination is associated rather with Bounderby and his extraordinary and highly imaginative creation of his past as a young vagabond 'born in a ditch' (59).

THE TWO MEANINGS OF FANCY

These considerations lead directly to an *ideological confusion* in *Hard Times*. On the one hand, the plot (and the metaphors) clearly suggest that constriction and turbulence, what Stephen calls the 'muddle' of the utilitarian worlds, can be transformed into 'order' by adding feelings and moral values. This is the novel's covert message, a revolutionary message, since adding a moral and emotional dimension would necessarily amount to a negation of the established system of utilitarianism, based as it is on the principles of cold-hearted calculation and self-interest.

ideological confusion

As such, the radical message contrasts sharply with the narrator's overt ideological stance:

Is it possible, I wonder, that there was any analogy between the case of the Coketown population and the case of the little Gradgrinds? Surely, none of us in our sober senses and acquainted with figures, are to be told at this time of day, that one of the foremost elements in the existence of the Coketown working people had been for scores of years, deliberately set at nought? That there was any Fancy in them demanding to be brought into healthy existence instead of struggling on in convulsions? That exactly in the ratio as they worked long and monotonously, the craving grew within them for some physical relief – some relaxation, encouraging good humour and good spirits, and giving them a vent – some recognized holiday, though it were but for an honest dance to a stirring band of music – some occasional light pie in which even M'Choakumchild had no finger – which craving must and would be satisfied aright, or must and would inevitably go wrong, until the laws of the Creation were repealed?

(67–8)

The narrator here limits himself to fancy in the sense of imagination; he seems to suggest that we should try to preserve the social status quo, and that the simplest way of doing it would be to add an imaginative dimension to the workers' lives. Many critics of Dickens' novel have objected to this *panem-et-circenses* type of argument – the twentieth-century equivalent of which might be to say that if workers protest they should be given a colour TV and then they will be happy. However, these critics may have condemned *Hard Times* prematurely: they have only seen its narrator's overt ideology, but have remained unaware of the covert ideology of *Hard Times*. We believe that what ensures the lasting appeal of *Hard Times* is precisely the existence of ideological difference, the tension between the narrator's explicitly stated ideology and his implicit radical ideology, as revealed by our analysis of some key metaphors in the novel.

PROJECT WORK: VICTORIAN IDEOLOGIES

a) Could the ideological confusion of *Hard Times* be due at least partly to problems of censorship or other social restrictions that Victorian writers were faced with? Do you agree with the critic John Holloway when he says that Dickens was 'a man whose outlook was amiable and generous, though it partook a little of the shallowness of the merely topical, and the defects of the bourgeois – the word is not too harsh – Philistine' (1962: 169–70)?

b) The opposition between a dominant (often conservative) and a muted (often radical) ideology is quite common in Victorian writing. In particular, feminist critics have noted such an opposition in Victorian women's writing. Read some Victorian novels by women writers and see if you can detect any such ideological tensions. For instance, you could look at Charlotte Brontë's *Jane Eyre*: what are the more conservative elements of Charlotte Brontë's ideology as it is embodied in the novel, and what are the more radical elements? The latter would include Jane's moments of uncontrollable anger and rebellion, which connect her with the ferocious figure of Bertha Rochester, the madwoman in the attic. (For more information about *Jane Eyre* turn to the next chapter, where we present a brief analysis of *Wide Sargasso Sea*, Jean Rhys' brilliant re-writing of the story of Bertha Rochester.)

ACTIVITY: POETIC METAPHORS

Analyse the metaphors in any of the poems reproduced in this book. Good examples for analysis and interpretation might be the personifications in the second quatrain of Wordsworth's 'The World Is Too Much With Us' (quoted on p. 33) or the dehumanizing metaphors at the beginning of Shelley's 'Sonnet to England in 1819' (p. 36). Try to make as explicit as possible what is being compared to what, and what the 'grounds' of the comparisons are. Also discuss the thematic and/or ideological effects of the metaphors.

PROJECT WORK: UTILITARIANISM IN LITERATURE

Utilitarianism is a highly influential philosophical and economic theory developed at the beginning of the nineteenth century by (among others) Jeremy Bentham in an attempt to solve the glaring social problems caused by the Industrial Revolution. Utilitarians hoped to achieve the greatest happiness for the greatest number of people by focusing on practical problems and by strictly applying Bentham's purely logical 'principle of utility'.

Compare Dickens' critique of utilitarianism with that of Aldous Huxley in *Brave New World* or T.F. Powys in his short story 'The Bucket and the Rope'. The utilitarian character in *Brave New World* is the benevolent dictator Mustapha Mond, and in Powys' story the utilitarians are, surprisingly or perhaps not so surprisingly, a bucket and a rope.

PROJECT WORK: CONDITION-OF-ENGLAND NOVELS

Novels such as *Hard Times* are often called 'condition-of-England' novels, because they deal with social problems faced by the English society of their time. An early twentieth-century condition-of-England novel is, for example, E.M. Forster's *Howards End*. Compare the two novels and, in particular, consider how E.M. Forster's novel reinterprets Dickens' fact–fancy distinction in more psychological terms: the world of fact (here, of the Wilcoxes) is equated with the superficial, outer self and the world of fancy (here, of the Schlegel sisters) with the deep, inner self.

Moreover, Forster sets out to show that these two worlds, and two aspects of our self, need to be integrated or 'connected' ('Only connect' is the subtitle of the novel). Examine what different types of connections Forster's characters (e.g. Margaret and Helen Schlegel, Leonard Bast) seek to establish and to what extent they are successful at this.

PROJECT WORK: MENTAL WALLS – A CASE STUDY

Walls can be not just literal or physical but also metaphorical or mental. We have seen how the mental walls of utilitarianism set up by Gradgrind & Co. imprison and restrict the Coketown people. You might want to listen to the songs of the Pink Floyd album *The Wall* and consider how they exploit the symbolism of walls. Are the walls symbols of limitations, conformity, protection, exclusion, imprisonment, isolation, or what? If possible, you could also read Robert Frost's poem 'Mending Wall' and discuss what its speaker sees as the positive and negative aspects of walls. Or take notes on the theme of walls and boundaries in Jean Rhys' *Wide Sargasso Sea* (see chapter 9).

Herman Melville's short story 'Bartleby' (1856) is subtitled 'A Story of Wall Street'. Wall Street is the financial centre of New York, but there is also a deeper symbolism of walls. Examine the symbolism in the following extracts from the story.

a) The lawyer's chambers, where Bartleby is about to take up employment as a scrivener (or copyist), are described as follows:

At one end, they looked upon the white wall of the interior of a spacious sky-light shaft, penetrating the building from top to bottom.

This view might have been considered rather tame than otherwise, deficient in what landscape painters call 'life'. But, if so, the view from the other end of my chambers offered, at least, a contrast, if nothing more. In that direction, my windows commanded an unobstructed view of a lofty brick wall, black by age and everlasting shade.

(76)

In fact, when Bartleby starts working in this office, he seems to be totally walled-in:

I placed his desk close up to a small side-window in that part of the room, a window which originally had afforded a lateral view of certain grimy back-yards and bricks, but which, owing to subsequent erections, commanded at present no view at all, though it gave some light. Within three feet of the panes was a wall, and the light came down from far above, between two lofty buildings, as from a very small opening in a dome. Still further to a satisfactory arrangement, I procured a high green folding-screen, which might entirely isolate Bartleby from my sight, though not remove him from my voice.

(82)

b) Gradually, Bartleby stops doing any work at all, replying 'I would prefer not to' to every request of the lawyer's. He spends his days looking at the wall:

For long periods he would stand looking out, at his pale window behind the screen, upon the dead brick wall. . . . I might know, from his long-continued motionlessness, that behind his screen he must be standing in one of those dead-wall reveries of his. . . . The next day I noticed that Bartleby did nothing but stand at his window in his dead-wall revery.

(93, 96)

c) Finally, Bartleby is forcibly removed from the office and taken to the Tombs, the New York prison, where the lawyer visits him twice before he (Bartleby) dies:

And so I found him there, standing all alone in the quietest of the yards, his face towards a high wall. . . . The yard was entirely quiet. It was not accessible to the common prisoners. The surrounding walls, of amazing thickness, kept off all sounds behind them. The Egyptian character of the masonry weighed upon me with its gloom. But a soft imprisoned turf grew under foot. The heart of the eternal pyramids, it seemed, wherein, by some strange magic, through the clefts, grass-seed, dropped by birds, had sprung.

Strangely huddled at the base of the wall, his knees drawn up, and lying on his side, his head touching the cold stones, I saw the wasted Bartleby.

(109, 111)

What could the archetypal or symbolic figure of Bartleby represent: is he an alter ego figure, embodying the lawyer's dark, irrational self? Is he an image of the author, Herman Melville, and the latter's wretched situation as an unsuccessful writer in nineteenth-century American society? Or perhaps a portrait of Melville's contemporary, the writer and philosopher Henry David Thoreau, who withdrew from society and, like Bartleby, took up an attitude of passive resistance against it?

When you have finished thinking about Bartleby and the symbolism of walls, please turn to the actual case study that we would like you to engage in: choose another image that informs a particular (literary or non-literary) text and study the symbolic implications attached to it by the writer. For example, you could analyse the image of the journey (physical and/or psychological?) in 'Young Goodman Brown', a short story by Melville's contemporary Nathaniel Hawthorne.

REFERENCES AND SUGGESTIONS FOR FURTHER READING

Page references are to the (1969) Penguin English Library edition of *Hard Times*. For a lucid introduction to metaphors and how to analyse them, see Geoffrey Leech's *A Linguistic Guide to English Poetry* (Longman, 1969, Chapter 9). A more challenging but also more difficult, language-oriented approach is George Lakoff and Mark Turner's *More Than Cool Reason: A Field Guide to Poetic Metaphor* (University of Chicago Press, 1989). They see metaphor as a way of thinking about one area of experience ('the target domain') in terms of another ('the source domain'). For a simple introduction to this approach and an application to a short story by Doris Lessing, see Jean Jacques Weber's chapter in Peter Verdonk and J.J. Weber (eds) *Twentieth-Century Fiction: From Text to Context* (Routledge, 1995).

The John Holloway quote in 'Project Work: Victorian Ideologies' is taken from John Gross and Gabriel Pearson (eds) *Dickens and the Twentieth Century* (Routledge and Kegan Paul, 1962). For further information about dominant and muted ideologies, see Sara Mills and Lynne Pearce's excellent introduction to feminist literary theory and practice *Feminist Readings/ Feminists Reading* (Prentice-Hall, 1996) and references therein. Essential reading for any project work dealing with *Jane Eyre* would be Sandra Gilbert and Susan Gubar's *The Madwoman in the Attic: The Woman Writer and the Nineteenth-Century Literary Imagination* (Yale University Press, 1979), which contains a brilliant feminist reading of Bertha Rochester (the madwoman in the attic) as Jane Eyre's dark double.

Finally, the quotes from Melville's 'Bartleby' are taken from James Cochrane (ed.) *The Penguin Book of American Short Stories* (Penguin, 1969: 75–112). Hawthorne's 'Young Goodman Brown' is included in the same volume.

9

LAUGHTER IN PATRIARCHY
AND COLONIALISM
Lexical Repetition and Jean Rhys'
Wide Sargasso Sea

Didn't she (forgiven) betray me
Once more – and then again
Unrepentant – laughing?
   (Rhys, 'Obeah Night', 1964)

foregrounding

Human beings seem to have an innate ability to distinguish between foreground and background. For example, when we look at a painting, certain details will attract our attention, they seem to stand out against a background of other things: we can say that these salient features are *foregrounded*. Similarly, when we read a poem or a narrative, certain features of the verbal texture will seem more prominent than others. It does not matter whether the writer intended these textual patterns to be foregrounded, nor should we be surprised if different readers notice different patterns. What matters is that the patterns that strike us as being foregrounded act as cues guiding our process of interpretation. They afford us a 'way into' the thematic complexities of the literary text.

FOR DISCUSSION

How do you see the role of the reader in the construction of the meaning of a text? Is it a purely passive and reproductive role, or a more active and creative one?

lexical repetition

In this chapter we shall be concerned with one particular type of foregrounding: *lexical repetition*. Obviously, it would be impossible to try to specify how often a word has to be repeated in a particular text before the reader feels it to be foregrounded. Indeed this depends not only on each individual reader, but it is also very much a matter of genre and style: a colloquial item in a highly formal text could stand out even if it is not repeated at all. On the other hand, the repetition might simply be due to a fairly lax and careless style. But especially in a literary text the reader will at least initially give it the benefit of doubt and raise the question of thematic relevance: is the repetition of this item thematically motivated? If this question is answered in the affirmative, then the reader might pay more attention to the lexical patterning of the text: where do we find the most significant occurrences of this item? does it occur mostly in the narrator's discourse or a particular character's discourse? in descriptive or narrative passages? The reader might also investigate the semantic loading of the item: is it used throughout the text in more or less the same sense, or in different senses? What connotations gradually accrue to its meaning as a result of its being used in so many different contexts? These are some of the questions that will be raised in the analysis below.

Charlotte Brontë's famous Victorian novel is the classic story of the governess, Jane Eyre, who falls in love with her employer, Mr Rochester, but then finds out that he is already married. Rochester's West-Indian-born wife Bertha, however, is a madwoman who is kept locked up in the attic of Thornfield Hall. Rochester's treatment of his wife reveals the hypocrisy of a *patriarchal* society, a society where women are considered to be different from, and inferior to, men. Indeed, he expects Jane to forgive him for his errors of dissipation, though he himself has never forgiven Bertha for similar errors. He implies that if a woman commits such errors, then it is not mere 'dissipation' but actual 'debauchery' (338), and that cannot be forgiven! Moreover, Bertha is not English but West Indian, and so Rochester describes her as uncivilized, bestial and subhuman, an 'Indian Messalina' (338), in a blatant *colonialist* and imperialist assumption of racial superiority. But, in spite of all his protestations, Jane decides to leave him and it is not until the end of the novel, when Bertha sets fire to the house, killing herself and maiming Rochester, that Jane and Rochester are eventually united.

JANE EYRE (1847)

patriarchy

colonialism

Why, you may wonder, did Rochester marry Bertha in the first place? Their marriage was an arranged marriage and he only met Bertha a short time before the wedding took place. Rochester was the younger son and, according to the right of primogeniture (the right of the first-born son), his elder brother was to be the sole inheritor of his father's estate, and Rochester would be left almost destitute. As a result of this unjust law, many younger sons turned into fortune-hunters, on the look-out for rich heiresses. In Rochester's case, his father had arranged his marriage to Bertha, as a consequence of which Rochester got a dowry of £30,000. This sum in fact constituted more or less the whole of Bertha's wealth, which she had inherited from her father. Thus she ended up wholly dependent on Rochester in economic terms as well as in other ways.

OF DOWRIES AND THE RIGHT OF PRIMOGENITURE

These sordid financial details, however, are backgrounded in Charlotte Brontë's narrative, which on the whole asks us to empathize with Jane and Rochester, and to turn in disgust from the mad and degenerate, animal-like Bertha. It is only Jean Rhys who, in her rewriting of the narrative material from Bertha's point of view, has effectively inverted the foreground–background relations of the original text and has brought out into the open the largely repressed subtext of racial prejudice, women's oppression and their interconnections.

JEAN RHYS AND WIDE SARGASSO SEA (1966)

Jean Rhys is the pseudonym of Ella Rees Williams (1894–1979), who was born into a family of former slave and plantation owners in Dominica. As a white creole, she felt alienated from both worlds, the Caribbean and England. When she was already in her sixties and living in England, she wrote *Wide Sargasso Sea*, a novel which tells the story of Antoinette Cosway, alias Bertha Rochester, Rochester's mad wife. Rhys' novel thus gives a voice to the oppressed madwoman of *Jane Eyre*. Her story is divided into three parts. In Part 1, Antoinette describes her early life at Coulibri, a former slave-estate in Jamaica, where she spent a childhood of fear and loneliness. Like Rhys herself, Antoinette belongs to a family of white creoles, impoverished after the emancipation of the slaves and trying to survive in a racially divided society. Their financial situation improves when her mother Annette marries a second time, but the hostility of the natives only increases, and Annette eventually goes mad when the blacks burn down the estate house and her son is killed in the fire.

Part 2 is Rochester's account of his marriage to Antoinette and their honeymoon on one of the Windward Islands (Rhys's native Dominica). After a brief period of sexual passion, the two grow more and more estranged from each other and their love (or whatever love there was between them) turns into hatred. Finally, in Part 3, Antoinette recounts her last days in the attic of Thornfield Hall, where Rochester has kept her imprisoned since they left the West Indies. The book finishes with Antoinette leaving her room to set fire to Thornfield Hall in a final act of defiance and revenge.

One striking feature of Rhys' novel is the frequent repetition of 'laugh' and 'smile' (when you read this wonderful novel, you may well be struck by the repetition of other keywords, in which case we hope you will follow up and explore their thematic relevance along the lines suggested below). Below you will find a selection of extracts from *Wide Sargasso Sea* in which these items occur. We have selected passages which make sense without too much context and which deal only with the major characters of the novel. Please study the extracts and pay close attention to the different types of laughter being described.

[1] My mother usually walked up and down the *glacis*, a paved roofed-in terrace which ran the length of the house and sloped upwards to a clump of bamboos. Standing by the bamboos she had a clear view to the sea, but anyone passing could stare at her. They [the natives] stared, sometimes they laughed. Long after the sound was far away and faint she kept her eyes shut and her hands clenched.

(17)

[2] She [Antoinette's mother] would ride off very early and not come back till late next day – tired out because she had been to a dance or a moonlight picnic. She was gay and laughing – younger than I had ever seen her and the house was sad when she had gone.

(23)

[3] I was bridesmaid when my mother married Mr Mason in Spanish Town. . . . I carried a bouquet and everything I wore was new – even my beautiful slippers. But their eyes slid away from my hating face. I had heard what all these smooth smiling people said about her when she was not listening and they did not guess I was.

(24)

[4] Yes, what a dancer – that night when they came home from their honeymoon in Trinidad and they danced on the *glacis* to no music. There was no need for music when she danced. They stopped and she leaned backwards over his arm, down till her black hair touched the flagstones – still down, down. Then up again in a flash, laughing.

(25)

[5] 'How do you know that I was not harmed?' she [Antoinette's mother] said. 'We were so poor then . . . we were something to laugh at. But we are not poor now,' she said.

(27)

[6] 'Annette . . . They [the natives] are laughing at you, do not allow them to laugh at you.'

(35)

[7] Some of them [the natives] were laughing and waving sticks, some of the ones at the back were carrying flambeaux and it was light as day. . . . And I was afraid, because I knew that the ones who laughed would be the worst.

(36)

[8] We [Antoinette and Rochester] came to a little river. 'This is the boundary of Granbois.' She smiled at me. It was the first time I had seen her smile simply and naturally. Or perhaps it was the first time I had felt simple and natural with her.

(59)

[9] [In 9 and 10, Rochester remembers how he got to know Antoinette:] It was all very brightly coloured, very strange, but it meant nothing to me. Nor did she, the girl I was to marry. When at last I met her I bowed, smiled, kissed her hand, danced with her. I played the part I was expected to play. She never had anything to do with me at all. Every movement I made was an effort of will and sometimes I wondered that no one noticed this. I would listen to my

own voice and marvel at it, calm, correct but toneless, surely. But I must have given a faultless performance.

(64)

[10] 'But don't you remember last night I told you that when you are my wife there would not be any more reason to be afraid?'
'Yes,' she said. 'Then . . . you laughed. I didn't like the way you laughed.'
'But I was laughing at myself, Antoinette.'
She looked at me and I took her in my arms and kissed her.

(66)

[11] Her [Antoinette's] little fan was on the table, she took it up laughing, lay back and shut her eyes. 'I think I won't get up this morning.'

(72)

[12] All day she'd [Antoinette] . . . smile at herself in her looking-glass (*do you like this scent?*), try to teach me her songs, for they haunted me. . . . she'd laugh for a long time and never tell me why she laughed.

(76)

[13] She'll [Antoinette] loosen her black hair, and laugh and coax and flatter (a mad girl. She'll not care who she's loving.) She'll moan and cry and give herself as no sane woman would – or could. *Or could.*

(135–6)

[14] I tell you she [Antoinette] loves no one, anyone. I could not touch her. Excepting as the hurricane will touch that tree – and break it. You say I did? No. That was love's fierce play. Now I'll do it.
She'll not laugh in the sun again. She'll not dress up and smile at herself in that damnable looking-glass. So pleased, so satisfied.
Vain, silly creature. Made for loving? Yes, but she'll have no lover, for I don't want her and she'll see no other.

(136)

[15] I [Antoinette in Thornfield Hall] saw the sunlight coming through the window, the tree outside and the shadows of the leaves on the floor, but I saw the wax candles too and I hated them. So I knocked them all down. Most of them went out but one caught the thin curtains that were behind the red ones. I laughed when I saw the lovely colour spreading so fast, but I did not stay to watch it.

(154)

Most occurrences seem to fit into two basic types of laughter: a social and negative one, and an individual and positive one. Let us briefly go through the three parts of the book and point out the most significant occurrences of these two types of laughter. Part I presents Antoinette as an outsider in the Jamaican world, from which she feels separated by barriers of race and class. These barriers are upheld by a negative form of laughter, the laughter of mockery and derision. Antoinette and her mother are repeatedly the butt of the natives' laughter (passages 1, 5, 6, 7).

Another variant of negative laughter is the laughter of deception and hypocrisy. Here the mockery and derision is not shown openly, but hidden behind a false smile of friendliness. This false smile is associated with the guests at her mother's wedding (passage 3) and also with Rochester at his own wedding (passage 9). At one stage, Rochester had actually forgotten to put on his mask of friendliness and the true derisive ring of his laughter was revealed to Antoinette (passage 10). His feeble excuse that the mockery was wholly self-directed reassures Antoinette and thus seals her fate.

Antoinette herself, as well as her mother Annette, are associated with a different, individual and positive type of laughter, the laughter of gaiety and happiness, of naturalness and spontaneity (passages 2, 4, 8, 11, 12). But the smile of naturalness and spontaneity can also easily turn into the laughter of wildness and passion (passage 13).

Rochester is frightened by this excess of sensuality. He feels like an alien in Antoinette's world of intensity, of excessive colours and smells:

Everything is too much, I felt as I rode wearily after her. Too much blue, too much purple, too much green. The flowers too red, the mountains too high, the hills too near.

(59)

Rochester cannot bear too much reality, he feels a need for masks and barriers. He has been brought up in a world of restraint and repression, which destroys the spontaneity and wildness of passion:

How old was I when I learned to hide what I felt? A very small boy. Six, five, even earlier. It was necessary, I was told, and that view I have always accepted.

(85)

As a result, Rochester determines to break Antoinette's wildness and passion, to destroy her laughter (passage 14). He imprisons her in the attic of Thornfield Hall, where Antoinette's laughter turns from naturalness and passion into madness and despair and she herself turns into the madwoman of Charlotte Brontë's *Jane Eyre* (passage 15).

We can summarize the discussion so far by graphically representing the different types of laughter:

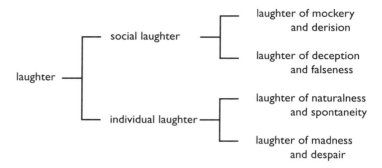

COLONIAL AND PATRIARCHAL IMPLICATIONS

Rhys builds upon the analogy that we noticed above in our discussion of *Jane Eyre* between the relations of men and women and those of the colonial power and the colony. Rochester is the colonial and patriarchal oppressor who uses his power to contain Antoinette's threatening otherness. A first strategy that he uses is that of labelling her as sexually promiscuous and hence mentally unbalanced – sexual desire being equated with madness. Another strategy is renaming her, thus trying to impose an alien pattern upon her true self. As a result, Antoinette is reduced to Mrs Bertha Rochester, an empty husk, a hollow shell of her former self, a ghost in the unreal world of Thornfield Hall. She has lost her inner richness, her power and her secret.

But at last, locked up in her attic room, Antoinette begins to sense that the other-imposed image of Bertha, which she has become, must be destroyed, burnt, consumed by fire; that she must break down both the false name (Bertha) and the restrictive labels (promiscuous, mad) of patriarchy. And so, in a climactic scene of simultaneous self-assertion and self-destruction, she jumps from the roof of Thornfield Hall towards her true self in an impossible wish for fulfilment.

Her suicidal jump is at the same time a final moment of insight and revelation, which consists in an eventual acquisition of full knowledge:

Now at last I know why I was brought here and what I have to do.
(155–6)

What she realizes essentially is that the magic, the power, the secret have to be preserved at all costs, and that her final defiant act of burning down the stronghold of patriarchy is the only way left to her of doing it.

But in *Wide Sargasso Sea*, this act is only a dream; for its 'realization' we have to go back to Charlotte Brontë's *Jane Eyre*, the text upon which *Wide Sargasso Sea* both depends and whose complacent imperialist assumptions it challenges. Such links between texts, whether of alliance or (as here) opposition, are called intertextual links or intertextuality, a concept which emphasizes the fundamental interdependence of texts (see also p. 51 above).

PROJECT WORK: PRACTISING INTERTEXTUALITY

In this chapter, we have looked at the repetition of words such as *laughter* in *Wide Sargasso Sea*. We could or should also have looked at Charlotte Brontë's use of these words in *Jane Eyre*: in particular, what kind(s) of laughter are associated with Bertha Rochester in Brontë's novel? Only the laughter of madness? Such a concern would already have moved us into the domain of intertextuality: from intra-textual to inter-textual repetition. But of course, apart from simple lexical repetition, there are many other domains of intertextuality, and hence also many other inter-textual links between *Jane Eyre* and *Wide Sargasso Sea*. Make a detailed study of all the connections and interactions between the two novels that you notice: from formal links (not only lexical repetition but also, for example, interdependencies in the types of imagery used by Brontë and Rhys – especially metaphors of fire) to the thematic and ideological interactions that we have only briefly touched upon in this chapter and that you should explore in much greater depth.

CONCLUSION

Our analysis of foregrounded lexis in *Wide Sargasso Sea* has helped us to identify some of the major thematic concerns of the novel. In particular, it has brought out a basic distinction between social or negative laughter, which can be seen as the symbolic expression of social and negative *power*, and individual or positive laughter, the symbolic expression of individual and positive power. Moreover, the image of laughter destroyed is used poignantly to suggest the position of woman as an oppressed alien in patriarchal society (see passage 14 above, for example). Rochester is the exponent of colonial and patriarchal power, who deceives Antoinette with his false smiles and finally traps her in the attic of Thornfield Hall; Antoinette, on the other hand, is associated with an inner power which allows her to shake the very foundations of the patriarchal order represented by Rochester. In this way, the analysis of lexical repetition has given us a direct insight into the dark core of Rhys's novel.

power

But of course we must be aware that there are severe limitations to our analysis, based as it is on a small number of extracts. Moreover, our exercise on *laughter* has been an exercise in *categorization*. But *Wide Sargasso Sea* shows us that categorizing and labelling is an act of shaping and often of mis-shaping, as is the case with Rochester's

categorization

colonial and patriarchal categorizing of Antoinette. So the novel reflects back on our exercise and undermines our certainties as literary critics. The ending of this chapter has to be as open as the ending of Rhys' novel.

PROJECT WORK: THE SECRET OF *WIDE SARGASSO SEA*

As we hinted above, Antoinette's suicidal jump is at the same time a moment of insight and revelation, in which she *sees* her whole life mirrored in the sky. Indeed, *I saw* is repeated no less than thirteen times in this final scene (154–6).

Throughout the novel, Antoinette is the one who *sees*, whereas Rochester tends to be associated with the limitations of *looking*. *Looking*, after all, is purely external, unlike *seeing*, which encompasses inner vision. To what extent can *looking* be identified with the colonial and patriarchal attitude? Is Rochester incapable or afraid of *seeing*, of embracing the alienness of Antoinette and her world? What is the secret of Antoinette and her world that Rochester is unable to *see* or penetrate?

ACTIVITY: GRADGRIND

Look at the description of Gradgrind in Charles Dickens' *Hard Times* (quoted on p. 107). Identify the keywords in this description and discuss their thematic implications. (For more information about *Hard Times* and Mr Gradgrind, read through chapter 8 again.)

PROJECT WORK: WOMEN AND MADNESS

Wide Sargasso Sea ends with Antoinette as the madwoman in the attic of Thornfield Hall. Study the theme of madness in Rhys's novel and compare with its treatment by other women writers. For instance, you could look at Charlotte Perkins Gilman's 'The Yellow Wallpaper', Doris Lessing's 'To Room Nineteen' or Margaret Atwood's *Surfacing*. Why do the female protagonists of these narratives go mad? Do the writers see their protagonist's madness as something negative or positive (i.e. a step towards psychic integration, self-discovery, authenticity)?

PROJECT WORK: POST-COLONIAL LITERATURE

Read some other literary works which display an acute awareness of the experience of colonization, decolonization or the post-colonial present. For instance, you could look at Caribbean writers such as V.S. Naipaul or Sam Selvon and compare their approaches to the problems of colonialism with Jean Rhys's in *Wide Sargasso Sea*.

You could also study how post-colonial writers often 'write back' to a canonical text of English literature, questioning and revising its imperialist assumptions. Jean Rhys, as we have seen, writes back to Charlotte Brontë's *Jane Eyre* in *Wide Sargasso Sea*. A good example for you to look at would be, first, to read Daniel Defoe's *Robinson Crusoe* and then contrast it with J.M. Coetzee's rewriting of it in *Foe* (1987) or Sam Selvon's in *Moses Ascending* (1975).

Page references are to the (1985) Penguin Classics edition of *Jane Eyre* and the (1968) Penguin edition of *Wide Sargasso Sea*. The epigraph is taken from a poem about Rochester and Antoinette which Rhys included in one of her letters.

REFERENCES AND SUGGESTIONS FOR FURTHER READING

Sara Mills and Lynne Pearce's *Feminist Readings/ Feminists Reading* (Prentice-Hall, 1996) contains an excellent, theoretically informed inter-pretation of *Wide Sargasso Sea*. For a colonial/ post-colonial perspective on the novel, see Hulme's chapter in *Colonial Discourse/Postcolonial Theory*, edited by Francis Barker, Peter Hulme and Margaret Iverson (Manchester University Press, 1994: 72–88). The standard introduction to post-colonial literature is *The Empire Writes Back: Theory and Practice in Post-Colonial Literature* by Bill Ashcroft, Gareth Griffiths and Helen Tiffin (Routledge, 1989). The same authors have also edited *The Post-Colonial Studies Reader* (Routledge, 1994), a comprehensive collection of key texts in post-colonial theory and criticism.

Finally, to continue your exploration of the phenomenon of lexical repetition as an element of meaning production, you could look at Verdonk's chapter in Peter Verdonk and Jean Jacques Weber (eds) *Twentieth-Century Fiction: From Text to Context* (Routledge, 1995).

10

POINT OF VIEW AND ITS EFFECTS
Resisting Brian Moore's *Lies of Silence*

narrator

Just as we make a distinction in principle between the speaker of a poem and the real-life poet, we also make such a distinction between the narrator and the author of a work of fiction. After all, we do not condemn authors for what their narrators say. For example, Jonathan Swift was not imprisoned for the suggestion made by the narrator of his *Modest Proposal* that the rich English families should eat the poor Irish babies:

a young healthy child well nursed is at a year old a most delicious, nourishing, and wholesome food, whether stewed, roasted, baked, or boiled, and I make no doubt that it will equally serve in a fricassee or a ragout.

(1729/1948: 551–2)

Swift's point is of course bitterly ironic: the way these destitute and starving children were treated was even worse than cannibalism. In cases where there is no hint of distance or irony, however, it becomes easier to identify the author with the narrator, and even to blame the former for the latter's views. Indeed, some Islamic fundamentalists would like to kill Salman Rushdie for the views expressed by his narrator in his novel *The Satanic Verses* (1988), which they see as blasphemously contemptuous of their religion and its prophet. In this chapter, we assume that readers can be critical of authors who do not distance themselves – through the use of irony or by some other means – from reprehensible or inadequate views held by their narrator, though there seems a world of difference between being critical of an author, and imposing the Islamic death-sentence or *fatwah*.

omniscient narrator

The question of the narrator is inextricably linked with the question of point of view or perspective. We can say, for instance, that Charles Dickens' *Hard Times* is told from the point of view of an *omniscient narrator*. Brian Moore's *Lies of Silence*, on the other hand, is told from the point of view of its main character, Michael Dillon. There is still a narrator who tells the story in the third person, but he

is a *limited narrator*: he limits himself to Dillon's point of view, so that **limited narrator**
the reader only sees what Dillon sees, only gets to know what Dillon
knows or feels. Limited narrators are more prone to being *unreliable*, **unreliable/**
thus leading the reader to question their judgements and values; **reliable**
whereas omniscient narrators tend to set up *reliably* the norms and **narrators**
values in terms of which everything in the fictional world should be
judged.

Note that these distinctions are not absolute distinctions but
continua, with different narrators being more or less reliable or
unreliable, omniscient or limited. A totally limited narrator might
only give us *external perspectives* of the protagonists; a less limited **external**
narrator might also give us *inside views* of one or more characters; **perspective**
and an omniscient narrator might allow readers an insight into all **inside view**
the characters' heads and reveal their most intimate thoughts and
feelings.

PROJECT WORK: *THE TURN OF THE SCREW*

These distinctions between omniscient and limited, reliable and unreliable
narrators are not just technical matters, but have an obvious influence on how
readers react to texts. For instance, seeing a particular narrator as reliable or
unreliable can lead to very different readings of the same text. A famous example
is Henry James' *The Turn of the Screw* (1898): whereas some readers see the
governess, its first-person narrator, as reliable and empathize with her in her
struggle against the forces of evil, others condemn her as a wholly unreliable
psychopath who is directly responsible for what happens to the two children. Read
James's novelette and weigh the evidence in favour of either interpretation.

Apart from the choice of narrator and narrative point of view, there
is a further problem here for writers: what language can they use to
reveal a character's thoughts? Traditional grammar offers only two
basic alternatives, either direct discourse (DD) or indirect discourse
(ID):

DD: 'Good heavens, what can I do?' Henry wondered.
ID: Henry wondered what he could do.

Neither of these two versions is very well suited to the expression of a
character's thoughts and so, in many works of fiction, we find authors
using a more flexible, transitional style which combines some features
of direct discourse with some features of indirect discourse and which **free indirect**
is usually referred to as *free indirect discourse* (FID): **discourse**

FID: Good heavens, what could he do?

a) **Which features does the FID sentence share with direct discourse and which does it share with indirect discourse?**

b) **More interestingly, whose voice do we hear in the DD, ID and FID versions, the author's voice or Henry's voice?**

DISCUSSION NOTES

a) Features shared with DD: exclamation, direct question with question mark. Features shared with ID: third-person pronoun, backshifted tense.

b) In direct discourse, there is a strict separation between the character's voice (enclosed between quotation marks) and the narrator's voice (Henry wondered). In indirect discourse, the narrator's voice has taken over and the character's voice has disappeared altogether. Free indirect discourse has the particular attraction for writers that it blurs the distinction between narrator's and character's voice: here the two voices seem to **the dual voice** merge into one, and two points of view are represented in one and the same utterance, which is why free indirect discourse is also referred to as 'double-voiced' or *the dual voice*. We can make a final distinction between free indirect speech, the use of free indirect discourse to represent a character's speech and free indirect thought, the use of free indirect discourse to represent a character's thoughts (see also chapter 7 for a discussion of free indirect thought in an extract from Jane Austen's *Emma*).

In what follows, we look at a novel, Brian Moore's *Lies of Silence*, whose narrative portions are consistently written in free indirect thought, and we critically examine the consequences of this technique on how the reader reacts to the text. The narrator limits himself to the perspective of the main character, Michael Dillon, and consistently presents the latter's thoughts in free indirect discourse. The reader gets no inside view of the other characters, only Dillon's external view of them: how *he* sees them, how *he* judges them, what *he* thinks of them. The effect of the use of free indirect thought is that readers are invited to sympathize or even identify with Dillon, and to take over his **co-operative** values and judgements of the other characters. Whether they do this **reader** is of course up to each individual reader: some readers, the *co-operative* ones, will indeed see Dillon as a reliable judge of events and **resisting reader** characters; others, the *resisting* readers, might keep a critical distance from Dillon and question his values. What we hope to show in the analysis is both how the technique (free indirect thought) strongly influences the reader to take up the co-operative stance, and how an analytic awareness of the technique helps us to, as it were, resist the seductions of the text and to read against the grain.

PROJECT WORK: IRELAND

Ireland has had a troubled history for over 800 years. Find out about the main events in the history of Ireland in order to understand the present political troubles in Northern Ireland.

Try and get hold of an introductory book such as Jill and Leon Uris' *Ireland: A Terrible Beauty* (André Deutsch, 1976) or Roy F. Forster's *The Oxford Illustrated History of Ireland* (Oxford University Press, 1991). Pop songs which deal with various aspects of Irish history (though in highly subjective ways) include Sinéad O'Connor's 'Famine' (from the album *Universal Mother*) and U2's 'Sunday, Bloody Sunday' (from the album *War*), and films include Neil Jordan's *Michael Collins* (about the events following the Easter 1916 Rising) and Terry George and Jim Sheridan's *Some Mother's Son* (on the hunger strike of Bobby Sands and other Republican prisoners in the Maze prison).

LIES OF SILENCE

Moore's novel focuses on the triangular relationship between a hotel manager, Michael Dillon, his wife Moira and his lover Andrea. The story unfolds against the background of the political troubles in Northern Ireland. The author seems particularly interested in Dillon's psychological dilemmas: first, whether he should save Moira, who is held as a hostage by the IRA terrorists, or the people in his hotel, where the IRA have planted a bomb; and later in the novel, whether or not he should testify against the IRA and more particularly, against one IRA terrorist, Kev McDowell.

POINT OF VIEW AND CHARACTERIZATION

Both characters and events are presented from the privileged middle-class point of view of Michael Dillon, the hotel manager. Thus Dillon's view of Kev as a 'vicious . . . bastard' (159), a potential rapist and murderer, is the dominant evaluation of the latter presented both in Dillon's direct discourse and within the narrative discourse as free indirect thought. The only contestation of the dominant view and the only alternative presentation of Kev that we get is in Father Connolly's direct discourse. However, the priest's integrity and hence also his view of Kev as a 'misguided . . . kid' (158) is highly discredited by the narrative voice in such passages as the following:

Dillon shook his head and sat down on the window seat, well away from this priest. He looked at the priest's raw, red face, his ice-blue eyes, his confident smile.

(156)

He [Dillon] looked at this stranger's red face, his anxious ice-cold eyes, his pleading smile, as he [Father Connolly] invoked that past, claiming kinship, here in a London park, to a man who did not remember him.

(188)

(Father Connolly is trying to convince Dillon that they went to school together in the hope that Dillon will not now testify against Kev.)

Use these two passages in order to illustrate Brian Moore's technique of characterization.

DISCUSSION

The priest, who turns out to be Kev's uncle, is presented as a sycophantic suitor, fawning and flattering in order to buy Dillon's silence. The two passages illustrate quite well Moore's technique of characterization: the repetition of a few salient features (here, the red face, the callous eyes, the ingratiating smile), which add up to a highly negative evaluation of the character. Note also the repeated use of the demonstrative (*this* priest, *this* stranger) with what Toolan (1995: 130) calls a 'reverse-deictic' effect: instead of denoting closeness to the speaker, the demonstratives here have a distancing effect, expressing the speaker's detachment from, and even opposition to, the character referred to. In this way, the narrative voice, which consistently presents events from Dillon's point of view, can influence the reader's judgements, against a particular character (Father Connolly, Kev) or, as we shall see later, for a particular position (e.g. Moira's stand against the IRA).

EXPLICIT EVALUATION

There is no need to discuss in detail the author's use of explicitly evaluative terms, since we have already seen in the previous section how the narration is coloured by Dillon's subjective perceptions and judgements, which the reader is invited to share. What we should like to add here is that this strategy is used not only in the description of characters but much more widely for the construction of a value-system by which everything in the fictional world – and, by implication, in the real world – can be judged. A couple of examples should suffice to illustrate this. When Dillon drives past the Maze prison, the narrative as usual presents Dillon's thoughts in free indirect discourse. Here is the final sentence of this passage:

It was a place where the false martyrdom of IRA hunger strikers had come to world attention, the prison the British called the Maze and the Irish Long Kesh.

(94)

As we read the novel, we become familiar with the evaluative stance shared by author, narrator and Dillon. Here is another example of free indirect thought from the end of the book:

There had been no war in his [Dillon's] life. He would never be called up as a soldier and put to the test of bravery in battle. He would never be asked to perform an act of heroism as a member of a resistance group.

(192)

Identify the explicitly evaluative terms in the two passages. Discuss the validity of the judgements made by Dillon on the basis of these terms.

What is striking in the first passage is the narrator's use of the explicitly *evaluative* adjective 'false'. Is this Dillon's judgement only? But it seems to be at least tacitly endorsed by the narrator, who nowhere suggests that this or any other judgement of Dillon's might be questionable. And yet what does a 'false' martyrdom mean? In what sense was the martyrdom of Bobby Sands and his fellow martyrs 'false'? After all, their suffering and death were real. So is it because they died for what the author–narrator considers to be a false cause? Or is it not the cause that is false but the means used to fight for it?

By the time readers come across the second passage, they know immediately that for this narrator the IRA would not qualify as a 'resistance group' performing 'acts of heroism'. Yet the criteria underlying such evaluative statements are nowhere made explicit: what are the differences between such present or former resistance groups as the IRA, the ANC, the PLO, the French Resistance during the Second World War, etc., and why would some qualify as performing acts of heroism but others not? More generally, what constitutes an act of heroism or bravery?

DISCUSSION

evaluative lexis

In this section we should like briefly to illustrate three strategies of implicit evaluation, namely the use of metaphors, nominalizations and presuppositions. First of all, let us look at a somewhat longer passage from *Lies of Silence*, which occurs when Dillon, himself a (non-practising) Catholic, watches his Protestant neighbour Mr Harbinson leaving his house:

IMPLICIT EVALUATION

Mr Harbinson, like ninety per cent of the people of Ulster, Catholic and Protestant, just wanted to get on with his life without any interference from men in woollen masks.

And now, watching him go off for his morning walk with his dog, Dillon felt anger rise within him, anger at the lies which had made this, his and Mr Harbinson's birthplace, sick with a terminal illness of bigotry and injustice, lies told over the years to poor Protestant working people about the Catholics, lies told to poor Catholic working people about the Protestants, lies from parliaments and pulpits, lies at rallies and funeral orations, and, above all, the lies of silence from those in Westminster who did not want to face the injustices of

Ulster's status quo. Angry, he stared across the room at the most dangerous victims of these lies, his youthful, ignorant, murderous captors.

(49)

A) METAPHOR

Analyse Dillon's metaphorical description of Northern Ireland being 'sick with a terminal illness of bigotry and injustice'. Consider the ideological implications of this metaphor.

B) NOMINALIZATION

nominalization

The noun 'injustice', which occurs twice in our passage, is a *nominalization*: it nominalizes a large number of concrete processes (or actions) and turns them into an abstract state, here a state of injustice. By doing so, it obscures or mystifies the different roles played by different participants in the processes. The reader is left wondering: who exactly is being or has been unjust towards whom and in what ways?

Examine each occurrence of *injustice* in the above passage and determine who the participants are and what their roles are (or were).

DISCUSSION

A) METAPHOR

In *Language and Power*, Fairclough discusses a newspaper article which describes social riots in terms of the spread of cancer. He argues that this metaphor implies a particular way of dealing with the problem: 'one does not arrive at a negotiated settlement with cancer. . . . Cancer has to be eliminated, cut out' (1989: 120). In the long quotation (p. 131) from *Lies of Silence*, the metaphor is used in the same way to suggest that terrorists and extremists have to be rooted out – rather than talked to, for instance as part of a peace process. Their values are constructed as the sick ones whereas, by implication, Dillon's and Mr Harbinson's values are 'healthy' – though what exactly these 'healthy' values consist in is a question we shall have to come back to. (In this passage they are only defined negatively: people like Mr Harbinson just want to get on with their lives '*without* any interference from men in woollen masks'.) The text also implies that the terrorists are the bigots and, the reader is encouraged to continue the inferential chain, they are the ones who commit the injustices. However, in the next subsection, we will suggest that there is a need to distinguish between two levels of injustices.

B) NOMINALIZATION

Is it only the injustices wreaked by terrorists that are referred to here? When we come across the reference to 'those in Westminster who did not want to face the injustices of Ulster's status quo', we may wonder whether Dillon is not thinking here more of the injustices of colonialism, of the oppression of and discrimination against Irish Catholics during the many centuries of English occupation of Ireland, and which continued in Ulster after 1921. And yet England is only said to be guilty of 'lies of silence', in other words, of not doing anything so that the injustices and inequalities in Northern Ireland continue. Nevertheless there seems to be a need to distinguish between two levels of injustices: the 'injustices of Ulster's status quo' have led to 'lies of silence' on the part of the British government, which in turn have caused the acts of 'bigotry and injustice' committed by IRA terrorists and other extremist groups.

The novel focuses on the latter injustices, where the IRA terrorists act against ordinary individuals and negatively affect their lives. It is on this level also that Moira takes up a stand against the IRA. This is presented as the 'right thing to do' (190), the position of strength, whereas giving in to the IRA is frowned upon as a despicable position of abject fear. Thus, on this first level, the narrative world is a world of actions and processes, a world which can be changed for the better or the worse, by different people engaging in different actions.

However, there is also the second level, where we are told about 'the injustices of Ulster's status quo' or, in another passage, about 'inequality' (59). At this level, processes and participants are never specified, never made explicit in the novel. Hence the second level appears as a world of abstractions and nominalizations, a reified world of states which are seen as immutable and beyond individual control. In other words, the political and historical dimension of the Northern Ireland conflict is *significantly* **significant** *absent* from Moore's novel, a glaring textual gap or silence. **absence**

C) PRESUPPOSITION

A related strategy of implicit evaluation that we briefly look at here is the use of presuppositions and other background assumptions, and we shall illustrate it by means of the following example:

There had been no war in his life. He would never be called up as a soldier and put to the test of bravery in battle. He would never be asked to perform an act of heroism as a member of a resistance group. He had, instead, been put to the test by accident, a test he had every right to refuse. And yet as he unlatched the gate and went up to the front door of the house he knew that the moment the phone rang and he answered it, the moment he told them [the police] he was afraid, he would lose for ever something precious, something he had always taken for granted, some secret sense of his own worth.

(192–3)

We have already examined some of the explicitly evaluative lexical items in this passage (such as 'heroism'), but here we focus on the last sentence, where Dillon wonders whether he should testify against the IRA or, on the other hand, back down and save his skin. He feels that backing down would mean 'los[ing] for ever something precious, . . . some secret sense of his own worth'.

What do we, the readers, have to assume about human beings in order to make sense of this utterance? What does it tell us about Dillon's view of human nature?

Again and again in this novel, Dillon and the narrator present highly tendentious views as if they were common-sensical and uncontentious, thus trying to get the reader to accept them as valid. The above sentence, for instance, presupposes that inside human beings there is such a 'secret sense' (otherwise it could not be lost). Ultimately, it seems to us, this presupposes a particular view of human nature, which the reader is invited to take over uncritically: Dillon's ideal is the individual fighter, the Rambo-type of hero or the lone bungee-jumper, rather than the civil rights demonstrator who makes a tiny contribution to the slow and unheroic fight against social injustices – and here we make explicit our own ideological allegiances.

IDEOLOGICAL CONTRADICTIONS IN *LIES OF SILENCE*

The cumulative effect of the strategies reviewed above (and of the overarching technique of free indirect thought) is to build up a theme or an ideology which, at first sight, seems quite progressive: namely, that standing up and speaking out against wrongs is infinitely preferable to keeping quiet out of fear, resigning oneself to one's fate, and thereby losing one's self-respect. *A Teacher's Guide* to Moore's novel puts this in the following way: 'To submit to a wrong because one believes that survival depends on keeping silent about it is to tell a "lie of silence"' (Lechler 1993: 56).

However, we have already seen that there is a need to distinguish between two levels of wrongs, wrongs committed on a social-personal level and others committed on a more historical-political level. On the first level it is the IRA that wrongs individuals such as Moira and Dillon; and here, as we have also seen, the novel advocates an *ideology of heroic individualism*. But wrongs have also been committed on the second level, whether it is the devastation wreaked by the English in Ireland for centuries or the discrimination against Catholics in

ideology of heroic individualism

Northern Ireland after 1921 – though these are present in the novel only as abstractions. Is standing up and speaking out against these wrongs not what the IRA are doing? In the long passage from the novel quoted above, Dillon actually sees the IRA as 'victims': 'the most dangerous victims' of the British government's 'lies of silence'. Why then are the IRA misguided and evil? Doubtlessly because they use violence and kill innocent people. We might therefore expect the novel to be consistent with its own ideology and to advocate other, non-violent means of redressing the injustices and inequalities of Northern Ireland's status quo. But here we will look in vain; on this level, the book utterly fails to advocate an alternative, positive programme of action. As we have already noted, the level-two world is presented as a reified world of immutable states which are beyond the control of individual human beings.

The only statements of policy that we come across on this level are of the following type:

Mr Harbinson, like ninety per cent of the people of Ulster, Catholic and Protestant, just wanted to get on with his life without any interference from men in woollen masks.

(49)

And people, ordinary people, would be sensible and see that their lives were more important than whether Catholics in Northern Ireland were given their fair share of jobs and votes.

(178)

But this of course means submitting to wrongs because one believes that survival depends on keeping silent or, in the words of the novel, being guilty of lies of silence. Here we come up against the *ideological contradiction* that lies at the very heart of the novel, and of which the author seems completely unaware: whereas, in the level-1 fictional world, the narrator enjoins us not to be guilty of a lie of silence, on level 2 the narrator is himself guilty of such a lie. As a result of this inner inconsistency, the seemingly liberal and progressive ideology of Moore's novel turns out to be a conservative, even reactionary one, which – with its stress on the privileged individual, who merely wants to get on with his life, whose only concern about the political situation is that he wants to feel unthreatened and unconstrained by it – ultimately reinforces the 'injustices of Ulster's status quo'. There is no attempt at a serious political analysis, no endeavour to put the events of the novel within the wider historical context and to work towards an equitable solution for all the communities in Northern Ireland. As such, the novel colludes with other oppressive discourses about Northern Ireland which see terrorism not as a political phenomenon but as a manifestation of irrational evil; and it perpetuates deeply conservative values and ideologies, which for centuries have been used as a justification for repressive political and economic policies.

ideological contradiction

ACTIVITY: GRADGRIND

Look again at the description of Mr Gradgrind in Dickens' *Hard Times* (quoted on p. 107). Does the narrator give us an external or an internal perspective of his character? What textual items can you cite as evidence for your view? What is the effect of Dickens' technique? (There are brief discussion notes on p. 137.)

PROJECT WORK: THE NARRATORS OF *WIDE SARGASSO SEA*

In her novel *Wide Sargasso Sea*, Jean Rhys uses a number of first-person narrators (see chapter 9). Part 1 is narrated by Antoinette as a child, Part 2 by Rochester, and Part 3 (except for the first three paragraphs) is narrated again by Antoinette but this time as a married woman imprisoned in the attic of Rochester's house.

Read our analysis of the novel again to remind yourself how Rochester, in order to preserve his colonial and patriarchal world-view, tries to contain Antoinette's threatening otherness: in particular, he renames her, and he classifies her as sexually promiscuous and congenitally mad. Antoinette, however, fights back against these restrictive walls and boundaries (both literal and metaphorical, physical and mental) that Rochester piles up around her. Interestingly, she even manages to break down the narrative and structural boundaries set up within the novel. Read carefully Part 2 of the novel and find the two places where this happens. Finally, discuss in what ways these matters of point of view are also relevant to the meaning of the novel and, more particularly, to our understanding of Antoinette's secret. (There are brief discussion notes on p. 137.)

PROJECT WORK: THE REPRESENTATION OF TERRORISM

Look at chapter 6 again on cultural stereotypes and then compare Brian Moore's representation of IRA terrorists in *Lies of Silence* with other novels about terrorism in Northern Ireland such as Bernard MacLaverty's *Cal* or films such as Neil Jordan's *The Crying Game*. To what extent do these representations reinforce or deconstruct cultural stereotypes of 'the terrorist'?

WHAT IS LITERATURE?

FOR DISCUSSION

Should Brian Moore's *Lies of Silence* be included in the canon of literary works, on a par with Shakespeare and most other writers discussed in this book? More generally, what is literature? On the basis of what criteria would you either include *Lies of Silence* in, or exclude it from, the category of *literature*? Should there be a separate category of popular literature? What would be the differences between literature and popular literature on the one hand, and between literary and non-literary texts on the other hand? How important a role does aesthetic pleasure play in these differences?

FOR DISCUSSION

In some chapters of this book (including this one) we have presented a more committed form of literary criticism. Should literary criticism try to be as objective and uncommitted as possible? Or does it only begin to be relevant when it deals with some of the worst injustices in our world: issues of gender, class and race? (Feminist literary critics focus on gender issues, Marxist critics on class and post-colonial critics on race.) Is it possible – and desirable – to combine these two aims of critical objectivity and social relevance?

Dickens does not tell us anything about Gradgrind's thoughts or feelings, which might have allowed us to empathize with him at least to some extent; the purely external perspective turns Gradgrind into a grotesque monster.

Gradgrind

Rochester's narration is interrupted by Antoinette's account of her visit to Christophine, her former maid. This constitutes an invasion of Rochester's linguistic space. But there is another passage in which Antoinette's voice actually manages to infiltrate Rochester's thoughts. It occurs when Christophine is talking to Rochester about Antoinette, and Rochester is virtually reduced to mimicking Christophine's words. A text-internal pattern is set up in which Christophine's direct discourse is followed by Rochester's thoughts in italics and within brackets. However, at the end of this passage, the pattern is broken when the structural slot reserved for Rochester's thoughts is invaded by Antoinette's voice (this is on page 127 of the Penguin edition of *Wide Sargasso Sea*).

Wide Sargasso Sea

This breaking down of structural boundaries announces the break-up of Rochester's rationality and foreshadows Antoinette's eventual subversion of the dominant patriarchal value-system. It also leads us towards a deeper understanding of Antoinette's secret which, it seems to us, consists essentially in the breaking down of all colonial and patriarchal boundaries.

Page references are to the (1990) Bloomsbury edition of *Lies of Silence*. The *Teacher's Guide to Lies of Silence* is by H.J. Lechler (Klett, 1993). Jonathan Swift's 'A Modest Proposal' is included in *The Portable Swift*, edited by Carl Van Doren (Chatto & Windus, 1948).

Michael Toolan's work on reverse-deictic effects is to be found in Peter Verdonk and J.J. Weber (eds) *Twentieth-Century Fiction: From Text to Context* (Routledge, 1995); Norman Fairclough's *Language and Power* was published by Longman in 1989.

The standard account for many of the intricacies of point of view is Wayne Booth's *The Rhetoric of Fiction* (University of Chicago Press, 1961), and a good introduction to free indirect discourse and its functioning in nineteenth-century fiction is Roy Pascal's *The Dual Voice* (Manchester University Press, 1977). More technical introductions to these matters include Paul Simpson's *Language, Ideology and Point of View* (Routledge, 1993) and David A. Lee's 'Language and Perspective in Katherine Mansfield's "Prelude"', in Verdonk and Weber, *Twentieth-Century Fiction* (pp. 113–25). Resisting reading is a strategy advocated by many feminist critics. They argue that female readers should adopt a strategy of resistance when reading male-authored texts. See for example Judith Fetterley's *The Resisting Reader: A Feminist Approach to American Fiction* (Indiana University Press, 1978).

GLOSSARY

alienation a term from Marxism, suggesting that we live in an unnatural state, in a state of estrangement from our true human nature, which is caused by the economic conditions of production in capitalist society.

alliteration a literary figure which consists in the repetition of an identical consonant sound at the beginning of stressed words. For instance, there is a /bl/-alliteration in Shakespeare's phrase 'with *bl*oody *bl*ameful *bl*ade'.

amour courtois the gallant code of chivalry regulating the love relationship between a knight and his lady. It was French in origin, but it spread to other European countries during the Middle Ages.

apostrophe a literary figure in which the writer addresses a non-human entity as if it could hear and speak and hold a dialogue, as in Keats' apostrophe to Autumn in the first two lines of his ode 'To Autumn'.

blank verse unrhymed verse, usually in iambic pentameter (see **iambic pentameter**). Blank verse was often used by Shakespeare and other Renaissance writers in their plays.

canon the canon of literary works is the list of those works which critics at a particular time consider to be of the highest literary or aesthetic value. See also **literature**.

categorization see **power**.

catharsis (adj. cathartic; from Greek *cleanse*) the effect of purification achieved (by audiences watching a play or readers reading a literary work) through the contemplation of how others experience pain and suffering.

defamiliarization many literary texts have an effect of breaking up the stereotypicality of our cognitive schemata, forcing us to look at the world in defamiliarizing ways and thus leading us to renew and revitalize our schemata. See also **stereotype** and **schema**.

deixis deictics are those elements of language which locate an utterance in relation to a speaker's viewpoint, especially in terms of space (e.g. this/that) and time (e.g. now/then).

denaturalization see **representation**.

double entendre a remark that is intended by the speaker to be interpreted in two different ways by different hearers: e.g. some of Captain Absolute's comments in Sheridan's *The Rivals* are understood literally by Mrs Malaprop and ironically by the audience.

epyllion (pl. epyllia) a miniature epic poem, such as each of the books which make up Ovid's *Metamorphoses*. In sixteenth-century England, it often took the shape of a short narrative poem which offers a burlesque version of a classical myth found in Ovid or Virgil. Shakespeare's *Venus and Adonis* and Marlowe's *Hero and Leander* are examples of epyllia.

evaluation (linguistic) is an important part of narrative, which can be marked by (e.g.) adjectives such as *heinous, wonderful* or verbs such as *accuse, praise*. Thus, for example, the sentence 'The teacher accused me of copying' implies that the teacher thinks that copying is bad.

feminine see **gender**.

foregrounding literary writers often foreground – or highlight – certain portions of their text by introducing either irregularities (deviations from some – usually linguistic – norm) or extra regularities (frequent repetition of identical or semantically related items, syntactic parallelism, etc.).

free indirect discourse see **methods of speech and thought presentation**.

gender a concept used to refer to the socially constructed roles for men (**masculine** roles) and women (**feminine** roles), whereas 'sex' refers to the biological distinction between **male** and **female**.

genre refers to different text-types such as the essay, the lecture, the sonnet, etc. These are not universal, but culturally-specific categories, which are often subdivided into relevant subtypes (e.g. Petrarchan or Shakespearean sonnet).

hyperbole a rhetorical figure which consists in an exaggerated statement that is not meant to be taken literally, as when Hamlet says:

I loved Ophelia: forty thousand brothers
Could not, with all their quantity of love,
Make up my sum.

iambic pentameter a line of verse made up of five feet (*penta* means five) in which each foot consists of one short and unstressed syllable followed by another syllable which is long and/or stressed. Here is an example from a sonnet by Edmund Spenser:

/ ︶ - / ︶ -   / ︶ -   / ︶ - / ︶ -   /
/One day / I wrote / her name / upon / the strand /

ideology a complex of ideas which seems to form a conceptual unit and which informs the way we think about things in a stereotypical manner. There are many ideologies in competition on certain subjects: for example, in relation to women, it is ideological knowledge which suggests that women stay at home and look after their children, when the majority of women in Britain in fact go out to work. At any particular point in time certain ideologies are **dominant** within a particular culture, and others are **muted**.

intertextuality a text is never produced or interpreted in vacuo, but always through our conscious or unconscious awareness of other, related texts. An intertextual analysis focuses upon these links between texts and studies the ways in which other texts influence the conditions of production and reception of a particular text.

irony meaning something different from what one says. The deep ironical meaning is hidden under the surface meaning and has to be reconstructed by the reader. For example, in Swift's *Modest Proposal* (discussed on p. 126), the surface meaning is 'Let us eat the poor Irish babies' and the deep meaning 'The way we treat these children is as bad as if we ate them'.

literature   a body of texts that are highly valued within a particular culture. Which texts constitute the culture's literary heritage and why they are highly valued are matters of heated debate. Thus feminist and post-colonial critics complain that very few women writers and post-colonial writers are included in the canon of English literature. They therefore prefer to use more inclusive terms such as 'literature (or literatures) in English'. See also **canon** and **post-colonial discourse**.

malapropism   the unintentional misuse of a word in mistake for one of similar sound: e.g. Mrs Malaprop in Sheridan's *The Rivals* says, 'He is the very pineapple of politeness', meaning in fact 'the very pinnacle of politeness'.

masculine   see **gender**.

metaphor   describing something in terms of something else. For example, 'threatening clouds' or 'sleeping flowers', where something inanimate is given animate characteristics (an animistic metaphor) or human characteristics (a personification); alternatively, human beings can also be given inanimate characteristics (a dehumanizing metaphor; e.g. 'the Hands' for the workers).

methods of speech and thought presentation   the main methods of speech and thought presentation are: (a) direct discourse, where the speaker's exact words are presented in quotation marks: *Bill wondered, 'Oh God, where have I put that brolly?'*; (b) indirect discourse, where the speaker's thoughts or remarks are reported by the narrator: *Bill wondered where he had put his umbrella*; (c) free indirect discourse, which is intermediate between direct and indirect discourse, combining the pronouns and verb tenses of the latter with expressive constructions characteristic of the former: *Oh God, where had he put that brolly?* Because free indirect discourse inextricably mixes the character's and the narrator's voice, it is also referred to as the dual voice.

mind-style   consistent linguistic choices made by a fictional (or non-fictional) character can give rise to the perception, on the part of the reader, of a mind-style, that character's particular and often idiosyncratic way of conceiving of the world.

narrator   the persona or position from which the narrative is told. The narrator of a work of fiction is usually first- or third-person, and can be reliable or unreliable, omniscient or limited. An omniscient narrator gives us inside views of the characters and reveals their innermost feelings and thoughts, whereas a limited narrator only presents the characters from an external perspective.

new historicism   historicist criticism attempts to put literary texts back into their historical, socio-cultural and intertextual contexts. New historicism is an important movement in modern literary theory, which has significantly altered our perceptions of (among others) Elizabethan and Romantic literature. See p. 35 for J.J. McGann's and J. Hawthorn's historicist re-readings of Romanticism.

nominalization   *invasion* and *oppression*, for example, are nominalizations of the processes described in *X invaded/oppressed Y*.

otherness   white males have tended to brand blacks or women as 'others', thus implying that *white* and *male* are the positive terms against which *black* and *female* are defined as their negative counterparts.

oxymoron   a rhetorical figure which consists in placing apparently contradictory terms side by side. Often used in the rhetorically-charged style of Petrarchan poetry to describe love as 'freezing fire' or 'burning cold'.

pantheism   the Romantics' philosophy or religion of nature is based on a pantheistic conception of God: that God is a divine principle which interfuses everything and can be found both in the world of nature and in the mind of man.

pathos   (from Greek *suffering*) the power of a work of literature to arouse feelings of sadness and pity in the reader or audience.

patriarchal society   a form of social organization in which women are considered to be different from, and inferior to, men.

pentameter   see **iambic pentameter**.

personification   see **metaphor**.

point of view   perspective or point of view is a key concept in literary criticism, but also one of the most confusing ones, as literary critics have tended to use it idiosyncratically. There is a need, therefore, to distinguish between the different senses in which it has been used: (a) there is, first of all, the question of 'who sees?' This is 'spatial' or 'perceptual' point of view, in other words the camera angle from which the story is viewed (or focalized); (b) There is also the question of 'who speaks?' This second concept of point of view, 'linguistic' point of view, raises the problem of the narrating voice. See **methods of speech and thought presentation**. (c) A further aspect of point of view is what might be termed 'cognitive' or 'ideological' point of view. Here we are concerned with the speaker's background beliefs and attitudes, and the ways in which they influence the nature of her or his perceptions and interpretations.

post-colonial discourse   the texts produced after the demise of the British colonial system, and which display an acute awareness of the problems of colonization and decolonization.

power   the ability of people or institutions to influence and control the lives of others. One way of exercising power is by **categorizing** other people as (e.g.) aliens. See chapter 9 for a study of the ways in which Rochester uses his colonial and patriarchal power in an attempt to contain Antoinette's threatening otherness. See also **otherness** and **patriarchal society**.

presupposition   when I say, 'The king of France is rich', I presuppose (or take for granted) that there is a king of France and I assert that he is rich.

Puritanism   the Puritans beheaded King Charles I and established the Puritan Commonwealth in England in 1649. For them, the only true king was God, who was in direct contact with every individual Christian. The Puritans also introduced very strict religious practices and moral codes, which were to be revived again in the nineteenth century during the reign of Queen Victoria.

reader   the reader can either go along with the text (co-operative, compliant reading) or read against the grain (resisting, critical reading). Feminist literary critics often advocate a strategy of resistance for female readers of male-authored texts.

reification   see **representation**.

repetition (lexical)   see **foregrounding**.

representation   how do writers construct the world in their texts? Some writers conform to mainstream conventions of representation, thus contributing to the reification of these conventions (they come to be seen as the only natural ones, the common-sense way of representing the world). Others, especially avant-garde writers, break through these conventions in an attempt to denaturalize them.

schema   cognitive schemata are sets of pre-structured actions which at a stereotypical level inform our thinking about certain spheres of behaviour. Many schemata, such as our background assumptions about masculine and feminine behaviour, are deeply imbued with ideology. See **ideology** and **gender**.

sentence structure   see **syntax**.

simile   an explicit comparison, often of the form *A is like B*.

sonnet a poem of fourteen lines, often in iambic pentameter. These fourteen lines are arranged according to a number of formal rhyme-schemes which organize the internal structure of the sonnet in two ways: (a) two quatrains (or octave) and two tercets (or sestet), as in the so-called Italian or Petrarchan sonnet; (b) three quatrains and one couplet (as in the so-called English or Shakespearean sonnet).

stereotype cultural stereotypes are the narrow, restrictive and prejudiced views of particular groups of people that are widely shared within a culture and that tend to attribute highly negative characteristics to these groups.

symbolism a symbol stands for something else, or suggests a range of other things. For example, walls can be a symbol of (among others) protection or imprisonment (see 'Project Work: Mental Walls' in chapter 8).

syntax the syntactic structure of a sentence can be simple or complex, coordinate or subordinate, loose or periodic. Literary writers often use an experiential syntax, which imitates or enacts the experience that is being described (see chapter 2 for details).

utilitarianism a philosophical and economic theory developed at the beginning of the nineteenth century by (among others) Jeremy Bentham. In *Hard Times* Dickens attacks the cold-hearted calculation and self-interest of utilitarian thinkers (see chapter 8).

voice see **methods of speech and thought presentation** and **point of view**.

wit originality in thought and in the expression of thought. For example, Oscar Wilde is famous for his witticisms, such as 'I can resist everything except temptation'.

INDEX

alienation 106, 118
alliteration 17–18
alternating rhymes 7–8
American Dream 84
amour courtois 22
apostrophe 22
Aristotle 68
Atwood, Margaret: *Surfacing* 124
Auden, Wystan Hugh 51; 'From Reader to Rider' 25
Austen, Jane: *Emma* 89–102, 128; *Mansfield Park* 77–8; *Northanger Abbey* 101; *Persuasion* 102
axis of volubility and of conventionality 102

Barnfield, Richard: *Cynthia* 12–13, 25
Behn, Aphra: *Oroonoko* 89
Bentham, Jeremy 112
Bergson, Henri 68
blank verse 7, 48
Brontë, Anne: *Agnes Grey* 78
Brontë, Charlotte: *Jane Eyre* 78, 112, 117–18, 122–3, 125
Browning, Elizabeth Barrett: *Aurora Leigh* 51; *Sonnets from the Portuguese* 23
Byron, George Gordon, Lord 35; *Don Juan* 68–9

canon 125, 136
Carroll, Lewis: *Alice in Wonderland* 78–9
categorization 123–4
catharsis 54
Cervantes, Miguel de: *Don Quixote* 13
characterization 90, 93–7, 101–2, 129–30

Chaucer, Geoffrey: *The Canterbury Tales* 51
class (social) 46, 52, 88–9, 121, 137
Coetzee, J. M.: *Foe* 125
Coleridge, Samuel Taylor 25
confessional poetry 41
Congreve, William: *The Way of the World* 78
conjunction (copulative, consecutive, adversative) 6
coordination 27–30
Cowper, William 25
crown sequence 2, 11

daemonic dream 83–4
Daniel, Samuel: *Delia* 2
defamiliarization 52, 88
Defoe, Daniel: *Moll Flanders* 32; *Robinson Crusoe* 32, 125
denaturalization 80
Dickens, Charles: *Hard Times* 88, 105–13, 124, 126, 136–7
Dickinson, Emily 51
Disraeli, Benjamin: *Sybil, or: The Two Nations* 88
dolcezza 9–10
Donne, John 10
double entendre 75–6
Drayton, Michael: *Idea* 9–10, 24

elegy 5, 24
Eliot, Thomas Stearns 51
enjambement 30
epyllion 51
Etherege, Sir George 78
evaluation 129–30; explicit vs. implicit 130–4

experiential syntax 31
external perspective 127, 136–7

Fairclough, Norman 132
Faulkner, William: *The Sound and the Fury* 28–9
Fielding, Henry: *Joseph Andrews* 78
Fitzgerald, F. Scott: *The Great Gatsby* 84
Ford, John: *'Tis Pity she's a Whore* 65–6
foregrounding 116, 118, 123
Forster, Edward Morgan: *Howards End* 113
Forster, Roy F. 129
free indirect thought 99, 127–30, 134
Frost, Robert: 'Mending Wall' 113

Gaskell, Elizabeth: *North and South* 88
gender 46, 52, 88–9, 137; and cross-dressing in
    Shakespearean comedy 76–7; in sonnets
    12–13, 24–5
genre 9, 24, 54, 68–9, 116
George, Terry and Jim Sheridan: *Some Mother's Son* 129
Gilman, Charlotte Perkins: 'The Yellow Wallpaper' 124
Godwin, William 36
gravità 9–10
Greene, Graham: *A Gun For Sale* 27–8
Gregory, Lady Augusta 82–3, 87–8
ground (of comparison) 104–5, 112

Harrison, Tony: 'A Kumquat for John Keats' 51–2
Hawthorn, Jeremy 35
Hawthorne, Nathaniel: 'Young Goodman Brown' 115
Heaney, Seamus 51
Heywood, Thomas: *A Woman Killed with Kindness* 65–6
Hilliard, Nicholas 11
Holloway, John 112
homo-eroticism 13
Hulme, T. E. 32
humour 9, 99–100; black humour 62
Huxley, Aldous: *Brave New World* 113
hyperbole 18, 73

iambic pentameter: *see* pentameter
ideology 74–5, 80, 107, 123, 134–5; dominant
    vs. muted 111–12; and metaphor 108, 132

incest 65–6
inside view 127–8
intertextuality 51–2, 123
irony 18, 76, 99, 101, 126
Ishiguro, Kazuo: *The Remains of the Day* 29

James, Henry: *The Turn of the Screw* 127
Jennings, Elizabeth 51
Jonson, Ben 68
Jordan, Neil: *The Crying Game* 136; *Michael Collins* 129

Keats, John 25; 'To Autumn' 34–6, 38, 51–2;
    'On Melancholy' 51
Kelly, Gary 102

language of the powerful 62, 64
Lanyer, Æmilia: 'The Description of Cookham'
    41, 45; *Salve Deus Rex Judaeorum* 49–51
Larkin, Philip 51
Lechler, H. J. 134
Lentino, Giacomo da 2
Lessing, Doris: 'To Room Nineteen' 124
Lochhead, Liz 51
loose sentence structure 27–30, 36

McGann, Jerome J. 35
MacLaverty, Bernard: *Cal* 136
malapropism 69–75, 78–9
Marlowe, Christopher: *Doctor Faustus* 65;
    Edward II 65; *Hero and Leander* 51;
    Tamburlaine 65
Melville, Herman: 'Bartleby' 113–15
metaphor 5, 89, 104–5, 112–13, 123, 136;
    animistic vs. dehumanizing 107–8, 112; of
    death 58–61, 66; in *Hard Times* 106–9, 111;
    and ideology 131–2
Middleton, Thomas: *The Changeling* 65–6;
    Women Beware Women 65–6
Millay, Edna St Vincent: *All My Pretty Ones* 24
Milton, John 37–8; *Paradise Lost* 32, 48–51;
    'When I Consider' 23, 28, 30–4, 38
mind-style 28
Montagu, Lady Mary Wortley 77
Montaigne, Michel de 58
Moore, Brian: *Lies of Silence* 126–36
Morrison, Tony: *Beloved* 89
myth 45–51

Naipaul, V. S. 124
narrator: omniscient vs. limited 126–7; reliable vs. unreliable 101, 127–8
nominalization 131–3

O'Connor, Sinéad: 'Famine' 129
otherness 80, 122, 136
Ovid 46, 51
oxymoron 11

pantheism 32
pathos 57–8, 62–3
patriarchy 102, 116–17, 122–4, 136–7
pentameter (iambic) 7, 17, 32, 38
periodic sentence structure 27–31
personification 5, 112
Peterloo massacre 36
Petrarch, Francesco 2, 6; Petrarchism 11–24
Philips, Katherine: 'To My Excellent Lucasia, on Our Friendship' 41, 45; 'Friendship's Mystery. To My Dearest Lucasia' 41, 45
Pink Floyd: The Wall 108, 113
Plath, Sylvia 51; 'Tulips' 40–1, 45
point of view 97–9, 102, 126–30, 136
Pope, Alexander 77
power 25, 62, 122–3
Powys, Theodore Francis: 'The Bucket and the Rope' 113
presupposition 131, 133–4
Puritanism 30–2

race 46, 52, 88–9, 117–18, 121, 137
reader (cooperative vs. resisting) 128
reification 80, 133, 135
representation 66, 88–9, 101; of death 54, 65; of the Irish 80–4, 87–8, 136; of women 51, 80, 89
Revenger's Tragedy, The 65
reverse-deictic 130
Rhys, Jean: 'Obeah Night' 116; Wide Sargasso Sea 41, 89, 112–13, 116–25, 136–7
rima chiusa, rima incatenata 6
Rossetti, Christina: Goblin Market 41–5, 52
Rushdie, Salman: The Satanic Verses 126

Sackville, Thomas and Thomas Norton: Gorboduc 54
schema (cognitive) 87–8

Selvon, Sam: Moses Ascending 124–5
Seneca 54
Seward, Anna 25
Sexton, Anne 51; 'To a Friend Whose Work Has Come to Triumph' 46–7; 'Old' 40–1, 45
Shakespeare, William 7, 136; Antony and Cleopatra 66; As You Like It 77; The Comedy of Errors 77; Cymbeline 77; Hamlet 54–61, 65; Macbeth 66, 69, 104–5; The Merchant of Venice 68–9; Much Ado About Nothing 78; Richard II 65; Richard III 65; Romeo and Juliet 13, 25, 54, 66; Sonnets 2, 6, 16–19, 37–8; Twelfth Night 77; The Two Gentlemen of Verona 77; Venus and Adonis 51; The Winter's Tale 66
Shaw, George Bernard: The Shewing-Up of Blanco Posnet 87
Shelley, Mary: Frankenstein 36
Shelley, Percy Bysshe 25, 35; 'Sonnet to England in 1819' 36–8, 102, 112
Sheridan, Richard Brinsley: The Rivals 69–78
Sidney, Sir Philip 7; Astrophil and Stella 2, 6, 20–3, 25
simile 104, 106–7, 109
Smith, Charlotte 25
soliloquy 66, 104
sonnet 1–26, 30–4, 36–8, 46–7
Spenser, Edmund 7; Amoretti 2, 14–18, 20–3, 25
stereotype (colonial) 80–9, 136
Sterne, Laurence: Tristram Shandy 29
Stowe, Harriet Beecher: Uncle Tom's Cabin 89
subordination 27–31
Surrey, Henry Howard, Earl of 2, 4–5, 7–8, 19, 24
Swift, Jonathan: Gulliver's Travels 77; 'A Modest Proposal' 126
symbolism 45, 113–15
Synge, John Millington: The Playboy of the Western World 83–8

Thoreau, Henry David 115
topos, topoi 11, 22, 24
Tourneur, Cyril 65

Uris, Jill and Leon 129
utilitarianism 108, 111–13

U2: 'Sunday, Bloody Sunday' 129

Virgil 46; *Aeneid* 7
voice: dual voice 128; in narrative 98–9, 101–2, 128–30, 137; in poetry 25, 31, 34, 48

Walcott, Derek 51
Walpole, Horace 68
Watson, Thomas: *Hecatompathia, or the Passionate Century of Love* 15–18
Webster, John: *The Duchess of Malfi* 57, 59–61, 63–6; *The White Devil* 57–66
Williams, Helen Maria 25
wit 9, 16, 52, 99–102

Wollstonecraft, Mary 36; *A Vindication of the Rights of Woman* 77
Wordsworth, William 25, 38; 'My Heart Leaps Up When I Behold' 33; 'London, 1802' 37–8; 'The World Is Too Much with Us' 23, 32–4, 112
Wroth, Lady Mary: *Pamphilia to Amphilanthus* 2, 11, 13–14
Wyatt, Sir Thomas 2–7, 9, 24–5
Wycherley, William 78

Yeats, William Butler 87; *Cathleen ni Hoolihan* 82–3, 88; 'Easter 1916' 83, 88; 'Leda and the Swan' 46–7; 'The Man and the Echo' 83

NOTES

NOTES

NOTES

NOTES

NOTES

NOTES

NOTES

NOTES

NOTES

NOTES

NOTES